Confederate Tax Census
for
Bertie County, North Carolina

- 1862 -

Compiled By:
The United States History Class 1975-76
Roanoke Chowan Academy

Southern Historical Press, Inc.
Greenville, South Carolina

This volume was reproduced
from a personal copy located in
the Publishers private library

Please direct all correspondence and book orders to:
SOUTHERN HISTORICAL PRESS, Inc.
1071 Park West Blvd.
Greenville, SC   29611
southernhistoricalpress@gmail.com

Published Windsor, NC 1976
ISBN #978-1-63914-335-1
Printed in the United States of America

We dedicate this research to Harry Lewis Thompson for his interest in and preservation of our local history.

Compiled By

United States History Class 1975-76

Roanoke Chowan Academy

Windsor, North Carolina

Lisa Barnes	Mike Lassiter
Rae Bragg	George Mardre
Donald Britton	Toni Mitchell
Ernie Carter	Emerson Orton
Brian Davis	Wanda Parker
Darlene Farless	Bonnie Perry
Sheila Farless	Flint Perry
Diane Hoggard	Sue Saunders
Robin Hoggard	Stanley Thompson
Terri Hoggard	Vic Thompson
Greg Knox	Victor VanNortwick

Ted M. Lassiter - Headmaster

H. Cullen Dunstan - History Instructor

Harry L. Thompson - Advisor

James H. Allen - Advisor

INTRODUCTION

Many people will remember the United States Bicentennial because they witnessed it: they attended its parades, enjoyed its picnics, and watched the more spectacular events of the country's two-hundred-year-old history re-enacted before their eyes. Other people, however, will more deeply and more fully appreciate the Bicentennial because they shall have been active participants in a celebration rather than the passive spectators of the festival.

The U.S. History class of Roanoke Chowan Academy is one group of active participants. They will not be among the passive spectators who witnessed a meaningless festival; rather, they will be among the ones who dug into the American experience, who criticized the American accomplishment, who analyzed and evaluated the American heritage so that they might join the debate to access the country's values, goals, and progress.

If there is one non-commercial benefit of the Bicentennial celebration, it is that on a national level there has been a gigantic effort to show the relevancy of American history to the citizenry. The importance of the study of American history is not limited to the founding of Jamestown, or the famous ride by Paul Revere, or the "tea party" in Edenton. American history is also the history of Bertie County and its people. In fact, the events, the attitudes, and the ideas of the county during the past two hundred years are probably the most relevant part of American history to the residents living here. But how many residents who walk the lands of Bertie County possess a knowledge and understanding of its history?

To encourage an interest and stimulate enthusiasm in county history, two local historians, Cullen Dunstan and Harry Lewis Thompson, have sponsored a Bicentennial project for R.C.A.'s American history class. The project was unique in that it allowed the students to participate in first-hand historical research studying and interpreting social and economic history of the area during the time North Carolina was part of the Confederacy. The result of this research in "Confederate Tax Census for Bertie County, North Carolina, 1862," and its value as a source of history is yet to be realized.

The book is a compilation of data from original tax documents listing land owners from various districts, slave holders, household goods and personal property important enough to be taxed, vehicles used for transportation, members of a family who fought in the Civil War, and residents who were eligible to vote. Although rudimentary, such information provides insight into the living conditions of the period, and how appropriate it is to focus a Bicentennial study on the era in time which is a midpoint between the founding of the country and the present age.

What contrasts can be made in the quality of life in 1776, 1862, and 1976? What progress is evident in those two hundred years? How have the values and needs of county residents changed in that time? These questions and perhaps many more can be studied and answered through the aid of the "Confederate Tax Census."

James H. Allen III

Table of Contents

Officials and Election Returns from Bertie County.............. page 5

Location of Districts (Bertie County map)...................... page 6

Windsor District... page 7

Salmon Creek District.. page 24

Trap District.. page 35

Indian Woods District.. page 46

Snakebite District... page 55

Hotel District... page 68

Jernigan District.. page 81

Durgan District.. page 87

Colerain District.. page 100

White's District... page 112

Explanation and Terms

Voter- 1 poll tax paid.

(150 a. $450)- 150 acres valued at $450.

Slaves: 39 ($13,309)- 39 slaves total value $13,309.

This list does not pretend to be a total listing of all persons and property in Bertie County for 1862. The possibility of missing districts for the northwestern part of the county does exist. The information listed was compiled only from the original documents available. Military rolls were not given for some districts.

OFFICIALS AND ELECTION RETURNS
FROM BERTIE COUNTY 1861-1862

The North Carolina Secession Convention 1861-1862

Delegates: James Bond, Samuel B. Spruill

"Election 13th May 1861 to elect two delegates to a sovereign state convention in the city of Raleigh on the 20th day of May 1861."

Samuel B. Spruill Esq.	354 votes
James Bond	398
Joseph Cooper	29
John W. Heckstall	28
Thomas Pugh	2
Lewis Thompson	2
H. P. Harrill	5
James Burden	5
Stephen A. Norfleet	2
Joseph Jordan	1

Voting Commissioners:

Hotel - 49 votes cast - Saml A. Bernard, John D. Griffin, John G. Fraim.
Salmon Creek - 118 votes cast - J. J. Rhodes, J. W. Webb, R. Pearce.
John W. Mitchells' - 40 votes cast - A. J. Dunning, Chas Stevenson, Wm. W. Thomas.
Colerain - 198 votes cast - Joseph White, Willie D. Hays, Edward Simmonds.
Mrs. Francis White - 46 votes cast - J. Pilano, W. L. McGlahon, George Webb.
Snake Bite - 68 votes cast - Calvin Pritchard, James Burden, W. T. Sharrock.
Windsor - 298 votes cast - Wm. Gray, James Duers, R. H. Smith.
Roxobel - 40 votes cast - Alanson Capehart, Jos. Harry, H. P. Harrell.

North Carolina Assembly of 1862-1864

Senators: Thomas M. Garrett. Replaced by David Outlaw (1862).

House of Commons: Peyton T. Henry, James Bond.

General Election for Governor 1862

525 votes for Zebulon B. Vance (Democrat)
105 votes for William J. Johnston (Republican)

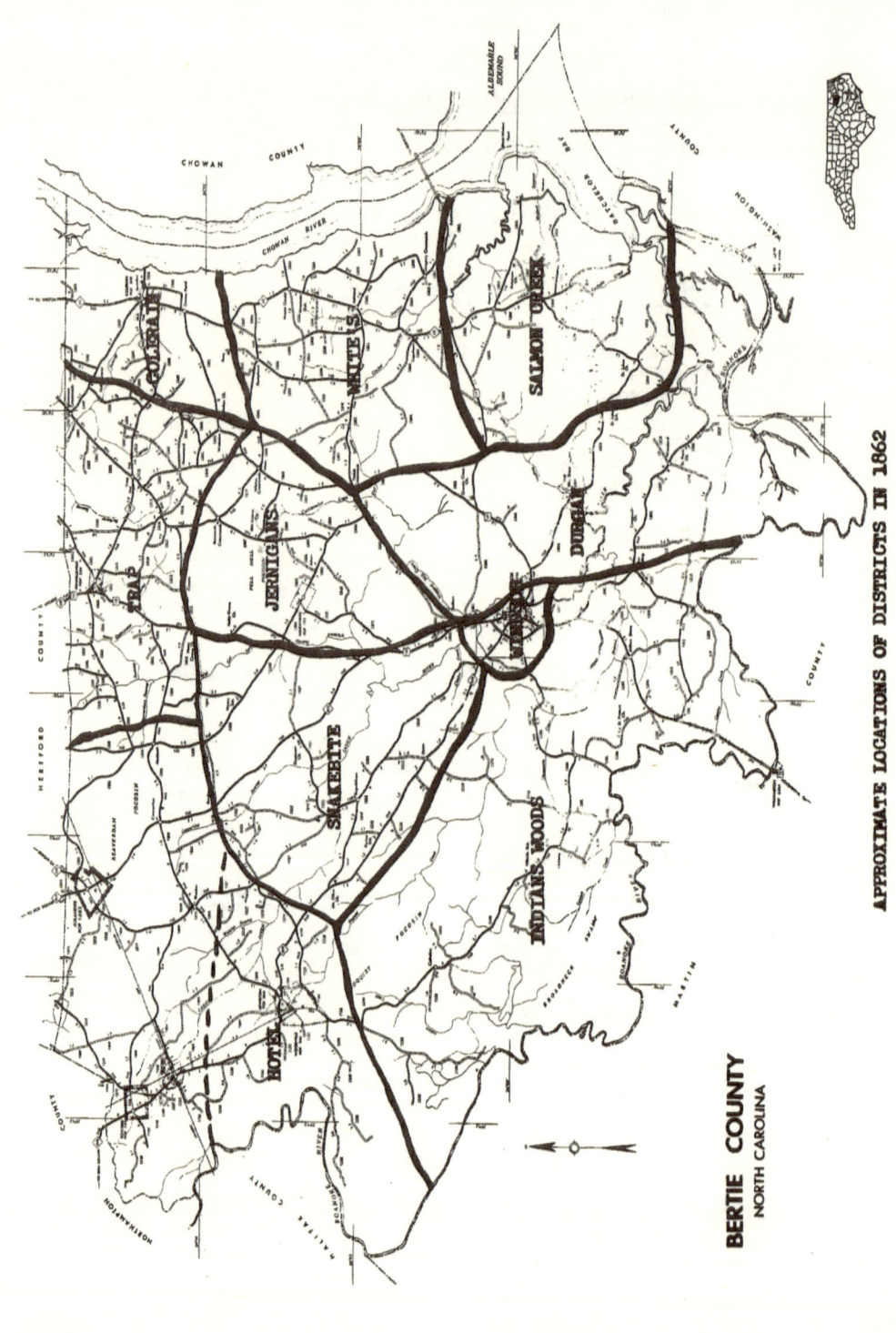

WINDSOR DISTRICT

ALLEN, THOMAS L.

    Slaves: 23 ($7500); Interest: ($5960); Gold Watches: ($40); Plate and Jewelry: ($74); Household Furniture: ($87); Pleasure Vehicles: ($160).

ASKEW, THOS. L.

ASKEW, WILIE I.

    Land: Marsh Tract 625 a. ($5000), Residence 320 a. ($3200), S. Gile and Swain Tract 70 a. ($350) (in Cashie Neck); Slaves: 43 ($17,200); Gold Watches: ($75); Pleasure Vehicles: ($200); Household Furniture: ($150).

BASS, PAYTON

    Land: 30 a. ($40); Piano: 1.

BELL, F. W.

    Land: 1 town lot ($150); Military Roll: "not given in".

BOYLE, MRS. M. C.

    Land: Rainbow 2000 a. ($10,000), Cashie Swamp 50 a. ($50); Slaves: 4 ($1100); Piano: 1; Plate and Jewelry: ($250); Household Furniture ($500).

BRANCH, JOHN, SR.

    Land: Durgan 160 a. ($320); Town lots: 4 ($2700); Slaves: 19 ($5700).

BUNCH, JERM., SR.

    Land: 1018 a. ($5000); Slaves: 23 ($6200); Interest ($4300); Pleasure Vehicles: ($60).

(Windsor)

BUTLAR, LEVIN

    Land: Wills Quarter (Residence) 300 a. ($400), Grayland 49 a. ($390); Slaves: 3 ($800); Interest ($440).

BUTLAR, MONROE (Mrs. Jno. Mizelle's dower)   voter

    Land: 30 a. ($30); Slaves: 5 ($1750); Silver Watches: ($15).

CAPEHART, B. A.   voter

    Slaves: 43 ($14,780); Interest: ($15,197); Bank Dividend; Bank of Wilmington ($650), Exchange Bank Virginia ($650), Virginia State Script ($750) ($67); Gold Watches: ($250); Plate and Jewelry: ($550); Pleasure Vehicles: ($125); Cashie Steam Navig. Co. "Steamer Alice" ($1050).

CARTER, WILLIAM   voter

    Land: Wills Quarter 75 a. ($75).

CHERRY, JOS. O.

    Slaves: 5 ($1500); Gold Watches: ($100); Piano: 1; Household Furniture: ($50).

COOK, WILLIAM, JR.   voter

    Interest: ($300); Silver Watches: ($20).

CRAIG, ANDREW M.

    Land: Residence and Mill 306 a. ($4600); Slaves: 14 ($5000); Interest: ($1200); Gold Watches: ($100); Plate and Jewelry: ($50); Pleasure Vehicles: ($125); Household Furniture: ($200),(Also paid for one free colored poll).

DEMPSEY, SARAH

    Land: Durgan 30 a. ($30).

(Windsor)

ESTATE CHARNEY CALE

    Land: 264 a. ($396).

ESTATE DEWBY WARD

    Land: 456 a. ($3900); Slaves: 24 ($9000); Interest: ($3400).

ESTATE MARY FLOYD

    Slaves: 1 ($700).

ESTATE E. J. MITCHELL

    Land: 1 town lot ($1500); Gold Watches: ($50); Silver Watches: ($10).

ESTATE GILES MITCHELL

    Land: Town of Windsor 90 a. ($90), town lot 1 ($800).

ESTATE MIKE THOMAS

    Land: 122 a. ($300); Interest: ($560).

ESTATE DAVID WHITE

    Land: 666 a. ($999); Interest: ($240).

ETHRIDGE, JN. H.

    Land: (Jos. Cherry Residence) 612 3/4 a. ($7500).

FALK, WILLIAM K.

    Land: Cashie Neck 600 a. ($3000); Slaves: 22 ($7550); Interest: ($11,613); Pleasure Vehicles: ($200); Household Furniture: ($100).

FANNING, THOS. E.   voter

    Land: near Windsor (Greyland) a. 34 ($425), town lot 1 ($2000); Slaves: 13 ($4300); Bank Dividend ($65) Bank of North Carolina; Gold Watches: ($50); Plate and Jewelry: ($80); Pleasure Vehicles: ($75).

(Windsor)

FLOYD, SAMUEL

    Land: Residence 340 a. ($2700), Roanoke Swamp 536 a. ($500), Aberdeen 600 a. ($1500); Slaves: 25 ($7000); Silver Watches: ($40); Pleasure Vehicles: ($150); Household Furniture: ($186).

GURLEY, WILL. P.   voter

    Land: Residence 6½ a. ($1500), near Windsor 37½ a. ($300), Indian Woods 260 a. ($2600); Slaves: 11 ($2130); Bank Dividends ($30) Bank NC; Household Furniture: ($25); All other property ($200); Military Roll: interest in vessel.

GRAY, WILLIAM S.   voter

    Land: 1 town lot ($2000); Slaves: 6 ($1200); Gold Watches: ($150); Plate and Jewelry: ($40); Pleasure Vehicles: ($150); Household Furniture: ($25).

GRAY, GEORGE

    Land: Residence 211 a. ($3000); Slaves: 17 ($5150); Bank Dividend ($325) Bank NC; Gold Watches: ($100); Plate and Jewelry: ($115); Pleasure Vehicles: ($200); Household Furniture: ($500).

GRAY, GEO. AND WILLIAM

    Land: 633 a. ($1500), town lots 1 ($150).

GRAY, GEO. AND WILL. AND PUGH

    Land: 2½ town lots ($500).

HARRELL, JESSE

    Land: White Oak Swamp 15 a. ($15), Roanoke Swamp 76 a. ($25); White Oak Swamp 150 a. ($125).

HARRELL, JOSEPH J.   voter

    Land: Residence 146 a. ($146).

(Windsor)

HASSELL, A. H.   voter

    Land: White District 60 a. ($100), town lots 2 ($2250), Durgan 90 a. ($150), Durgan 120 a. ($300), Roxobel 100 a. ($140); Slaves: 6 ($2500); State and County Officers: ($1500); Gold Watches: ($60); Pleasure Vehicles: ($50), (Also paid for one free colored poll).

HASSELL AND HOGGARD

    Land: Wills Quarter 25 a. ($25).

HASSELL AND SMITH

    Land: near Windsor 122 a. ($1070).

HAWKINS, WILL. H.   voter

    Land: Will Quarter 80 a. ($300).

HENSBERRY AND McGLACHEN

    Land: Durgan 30 a. ($30).

HENSBERRY, PETER

    Land: Bucklesberry 370 a. ($400), town lots 5 ($4500), Bucklesberry 225 a. ($225); Slaves: 8 ($3000).

HOGGARD, JOSEPH   voter

    Land: Residence 200 a. ($300).

HOGGARD, WILL. H.

    Land: Windsor District 220 a. ($2000), town lots 1 ($500), Whites District 400 a. ($600), Residence 496 a. ($1122), Colerain 314 a. ($400), Colerain 30 a. ($240), Piney Woods 50 a. ($35), Piney Woods 50 a. ($25); Slaves: 33 ($12,000); Gold Watches: ($100); Pleasure Vehicles: ($300); Household Furniture: ($150).

HOGGARD AND MITCHELL

    Land: Windsor town lots 4 ($4000); Silver Watches: ($100); Household Furniture: ($1000).

(Windsor)

HOLDEN, ABRAM   voter

    Land: Residence 100 a. ($300); Interest: ($321); Silver Watches: ($20).

JOHNSTON, JNO. R.

    Land: Late Residence 50 a. ($50).

JOHNSTON, LITTLETON   voter

    Land: Residence Wills Quarter 105 a. ($200); Interest: ($175).

JOHNSTON, MARCUS R.   voter

    Land: Pecosin 109 a. ($109).

JONES, RHODES

    Land: 1 town lot ($500).

JORDAN, MRS. MARANDA

    Land: 1 town lot ($800).

LEE, JOHN H.   voter

    Land: near Windsor 95 a. ($950), town lots 1 ($2500); Slaves: 10 ($4000); Gold Watches: ($80); Pleasure Vehicles: ($75); Household Furniture: ($50).

LOWENBERG, J. R.   voter

    Interest: ($3595).

MARDRE, GEORGE   voter

    Land: Roanoke 150 a. ($400), town lots 2 ($1000), Piney Woods 170 a. ($250), Holden and Mizills Land 400 a. ($800).

(Windsor)

MITCHELL, JOHN   voter

   Land: 100 a. ($100); Slaves: 2 ($800); Silver Watches: ($12).

MITCHELL, JOHN D.   voter

   Land: Wills Quarter 76 a. ($125).

MITCHELL, LAWRENCE   voter

   Land: Durgan District 150 a. ($300); Slaves: 2 ($900); Interest: ($600); Gold Watches: ($150); Pleasure Vehicles: ($100).

MITCHELL, AND MIZILLS

   Land: Mill on Wills Quarter 100 a. ($3000); Slaves: 1 ($50); Interest: ($780).

MITCHELL, WILL. P.   voter

   Land: 100 a. ($100).

MITCHELL, WILL. W.   voter

   Slaves: 1 ($700); Silver Watches: ($35).

MIZILLS, CHARLES   voter

   Silver Watches: ($10).

MIZILLS, GEO. W.   voter

   Interest: ($106); Silver Watches: ($15).

MIZILLS, JOHN B.   voter

MIZILLS, MRS. JNO. (see BUTLAR, MONROE)

MIZILLS, JOSIAH

   Land: Residence 360 a. ($810); Interest: ($495); Silver Watches: ($18); Pleasure Vehicles: ($50).

(Windsor)

MIZILLS, NANCY J. AND JOSIAH (INFANTS)

    Interest: ($76).

MIZILLS, MARY

    Land: 610 a. ($915).

MIZILLS, MORA L.

    Land: Wills Quarter 362 a. ($724), Wills Quarter 75 a. ($180); Slaves: 2 ($500); Silver Watches: ($15); Pleasure Vehicles: ($50).

MIZILLS, ROXANNA

    Interest: ($464).

MORGAN, SARAH E.

    Slaves: 5 ($1050).

MYERS, NATHANIAL

    Land: Piney Woods 225 a. ($300).

MYERS, PRESSELLA C.

    Slaves: 9 ($2700).

MYERS, WILLIAM   voter

    Land: Residence 230 a. ($260); Interest: ($100).

NEWBY, JOHN   voter

NEWBY, WILLIAM   voter

OUTLAW, MISS BELLIE

    Slaves: 2 ($800); Gold Watches: ($25).

(Windsor)

OUTLAW, DAVID

    Lawyer; ($1000); Gold Watches: ($100).

OUTLAW, DAVID, JR.

    Interest: ($507).

PARKER, JNO. AND MISS NEWBY (husband of Miss Newby)

    Land: 1 town lot ($350).

PHELPS, HENRY

    Land: 75 a. ($100).

POWELL, HENRY

    Land: Residence 34½ a. ($75).

POWELL, WILL. R. (children)

    Land: Residence 250 a. ($850); Slaves: 2 ($500); Pleasure Vehicles: ($100).

PRUDEN, WILL. S.

    Land: Residence 110 a. ($110), town lots 2 ($1200); Slaves: 3 ($650); Interest: ($2605).

PUGH, BENJAMIN

    Land: Residence 100 a. ($100).

PUGH, VICTORIA O.

    Slaves: 11 ($4000).

RASCOE, JOHN T.   voter

    Land: 1/8 town lot ($260); Slaves: 1 ($530); Gold Watches: ($100).

(Windsor)

RHODES, NEZERATH

    Land: Residence 100 a. ($300); Slaves: 7 ($1500); Silver Watches: ($15).

RHODES, WILL. G.

    Land: Durgan 206 a. ($412); Silver Watches: ($20); Pleasure Vehicles: ($50).

RICE, GEO. W.   voter

    Land: Cashie Swamp 200 a. ($400).

RICE, NAPOLEON

    Interest: ($1270).

RICE, SARAH F.

    Slaves: 4 ($1300).

RICE, WILL. D.   voter

    Land: Cashie Swamp 250 a. ($250); Interest: ($385); Pleasure Vehicles: ($100).

RIDDICK, THOS. W.

    Land: Cashie Neck 2221 a. ($12,500), Cashie Neck 200 a. ($2500), town lots 1 ($300); Slaves: 53 ($15,300); Interest: ($25,207); Gold Watches: ($50); Piano: 1; Plate and Jewelry: ($25); Pleasure Vehicles: ($200); Household Furniture: ($300).

ROULHAC, FRANCES L. MISS   voter

    Slaves: 58 ($17,400); Interest: ($670); Gold Watches: ($40); Plate and Jewelry: ($30).

RUSSELL, B. B.

    Land: 3 town lots ($2250); Interest: ($1850); Silver Watches: ($10); Household Furniture: ($100).

(Windsor)

RYAN, EMELY L. MISS

    Land: Crutchlow Fishing 200½ a. ($100), town lots 4 ($3000); Slaves: 51 ($15,000); Interest: ($5000); Gold Watches: ($100); Piano: 1; Plate and Jewelry: ($100); Pleasure Vehicles: ($50); Household Furniture: ($500).

SCURVIN, THOS. B.   voter

    Interest: ($700); Gold Watches: ($50); Piano: 1; Plate and Jewelry: ($50); Household Furniture: ($175).

SHADGOTT, SARAH E.

    Land: Cashie River 300 a. ($300); Gold Watches: ($60); Plate and Jewelry: ($50); Household Furniture: ($50).

SHEPERD, JNO. S.

    Land: near Windsor 18 a. ($500), town lots 1 ($250); Slaves: 2 ($0000); Interest: ($200).

SKIRVIN, GEORGE   voter

    Interest: ($200).

SMITH, EVA

    Interest: ($600).

SMITH, DR. R. H.   voter

    Land: Roanoke Swamp 200 a. ($25), town lots 2 ($2500); Slaves: 21 ($6300); Bank Dividends: ($98), Bank of N. C.; Gold Watches: ($100); Piano: 1; Plate and Jewelry: ($40); Pleasure Vehicles: ($50).

SMITH, STARK B.

    Slaves: 3 ($1200); Interest: ($10,000); Physicians: ($4000); Gold Watches: ($75); Pleasure Vehicles: ($100); Household Furniture: ($150).

(Windsor)

SMITHWICK, SAM. W.

    Land: Cashie Neck 1010 a. ($8600); Slaves: 38 ($11,050); Gold Watches: ($60); Silver Watches: ($75); Pleasure Vehicles: ($400); Household Furniture: ($50).

SPELLER, THOS. H.

    Land: Cashie Neck 1771 a. ($17,710), town lots 2 ($2000); Slaves: 89 ($27,000); Gold Watches: ($80); Piano: 1.

SPELLINGS

    Land: 1 town lot ($1000); Slaves: 2 ($450); Interest: ($500).

SPIVEY, JOS. B.   voter

    Land: Piney Woods 455 a. ($796), town lots 8 ($3390), Pecosin 150 a. ($185), Piney Woods 100 a. ($100); Slaves: 5 (no value); Interest: ($8498); Gold Watches: ($60), Pleasure Vehicles: ($50); Household Furniture: ($68).

STEELY, JAMES B.

    Land: 603 a. ($1809); Interest: ($575); Pleasure Vehicles: ($100).

SUTTON, WILLIAM W.   voter

    Slaves: 16 ($5600); Gold Watches: ($135); Plate and Jewelry: ($68); Pleasure Vehicles: ($50); Household Furniture: ($100).

TAYLOR, DAVID E.   voter

    Land: Residence ($1860), 60 a. ($300); Slaves: 3 ($800); Gold Watches: ($100); Piano: 1; Pleasure Vehicles: ($150).

TAYLOR, JON. S.

    Land: Residence ($1860), 920 a. ($4700); Slaves: 24 ($6950); Interest: ($1250); Bank Dividends: ($143); Bank Officer: ($875); Piano: 1; Plate and Jewelry: ($30); Pleasure Vehicles: ($150); Household Furniture: ($400).

(Windsor)

TAYLOR, ROBR. R.

    Land: Residence 1732 a. ($3390), in Mill and Pond 300 a. ($1500); Slaves: 18 ($5400); Silver Watches: ($25); Pleasure Vehicles: ($100); Household Furniture: ($200).

THATCH, STEPHEN

    Interest: ($200).

THOMAS, EVENRELLA

    Land: 106 a. ($500); Interest: ($425).

THOMAS, JOSIAH

    Land: 80 a. ($400).

THOMAS, L. CAPT.   voter

    Slaves: 1 ($400); Silver Watches: ($20); Pleasure Vehicles: ($50); Household Furniture: ($250).

THOMAS, MISS SARAH

    Slaves: 5 ($1250).

THOMPSON, A. R.   voter

    Interest: ($437); Silver Watches: ($30).

WALLER, NANCY

    Land: 1 town lot ($200).

WARD, MRS. SARAH

    Land: Residence 101 a. ($300); Slaves: 8 ($2250); Interest: ($800); Pleasure Vehicles: ($400); Household Furniture: ($100).

WATERMAN, MRS. ELIZA (taken from tax list)

    Land: 2 town lots (1 at $500, other at $800); Interest: ($1400).

(Windsor)

WATERS, CYRUS   voter

   Gold Watches: ($50).

WEBB, EDWARD   voter

   Interest: ($616); Bank Officers: ($875); Gold Watches: ($30).

WEBB, JOHN   voter

   Silver Watches: ($25).

WEBB, S. S.

   Land: 2 town lots ($1500); Slaves: 2 ($600); Bank Officers: ($2500);
   Gold Watches: ($50); Piano: 1; Plate and Jewelry: ($45); Household Furniture: ($50).

WHITAKER, JNO. E.   voter

   Land: Roquist 400 a. ($2000); Slaves:7 ($3000); Silver Watches:
   ($16).

WHITE, ANN

   Land: 75 a. ($112).

WHITE, BENJAMIN   voter

   Land: 150 a. ($150), 80 a. ($54).

WHITE, BRYANT

   Land: Residence Miles Quarter 286 a. ($300); Interest: ($100).

WHITE, BRYANT, JR.   voter

WHITE, JOSEPH   voter

WHITE, JOSEPH   voter

   Land: Piney Woods 100 a. ($100).

(Windsor)

WHITE, MARY

    Land: 75 a. ($112).

WHITE, REUBEN S.   voter

WHITE, STANLEY   voter

    Land: 645 a. ($625); Slaves: 6 ($1600).

WILFORD, ALANSON   voter

    Land: Residence Miles Quarter 210 a. ($315).

WILFORD, JONAH   voter

    Land: 150 a. ($150).

WILSON, TURNER

    Land: Pell Mell 2500 a. ($7150), town lots 3 ($1900), Gray Town 12½ a. ($180), Bird Track 25 a. ($37), Coleraine 11 a. ($330), town lot 1 ($1500); Slaves: 35 ($9775); Interest: ($5812); Bank Dividends: ($240) From Bank N. C.; Gold Watches: ($70); Piano: 1; Pleasure Vehicles: ($200); Household Furniture: ($250).

WINSTON, P. H.   voter

    Land: Terrapin Point to ----- 1200 a. ($4100), town lots 4 ($1900), Honey Creek to ----- 100 a. ($400), (?) Fishery (no acreage given) ($40), (Durgan) Riddett 100 a. ($150), Nicholls Land 251 a. ($502), Hardy (?) 50 a. ($10), Wilson Tract 100 a. ($100), Residence 258 a. ($3000); Slaves: 33 ($9900); Gold Watches: ($100); Plate and Jewelry: ($150); Pleasure Vehicles: ($250); Household Furniture: ($1000).

WISH, MRS. ELIZABETH

    Land: 5 town lots ($4000); Slaves: 26 ($7500); Interest: ($1878); Household Furniture: ($25).

WYNNS, MISS NANCY

    Land: (no name) 700 a. ($1500); Slaves: 4 ($1525); Interest: ($650).

(Windsor)

WYNNS, WILL. D. voter

    Land: Residence 1000 a. ($5000), 150 a. ($126); Slaves: 25 ($6000).

PERSONS ON TAX LIST WHO HAVE NOT LISTED IN THE ABOVE

BASS, THOMAS	MIZILLS, AARON S.
DAVIS, ALLEN, JR.	MIZILLS, DAVID B.
ETHERIDGE, JN. H.	PUGH, ISAAC
HARROLD, LEON CARLOS	SIMMONS AND WINSTON
HARRELL, WILL. E.	SIMMONS, ROB. R.
HOBBS, Q. T.	SAUNDERLIN, HARRIET
HARRISON, REUBEN	SPIVEY AND BRIDGES
ESTATE JNO. R.	TAYLOR, WATSON
JAMES, RHODES	WHITE, MEREDITH
LABRATAUX, WILLIAM	VALENTINE, DANIEL
BIGGS, KADER	CARTER, JAMES T.
MORRIS, WILL. M.	CARTER, BENJAMIN

"I solemnly swear that I have diligently inquired, and have no just reason to believe that there is any property on other subjects of taxation in my district not entered and valued where the source is required to be valid, in the above list, and the foregoing valuation in my judgment and belief is a fair actual value thereof in cash and that in assessing the same I have endeavored to do equal justice to the public and the individuals concerned or help me God except the people above reported."

Sworn and subscribed before me,   Geo. Gray Ass$_r^s$
    W. P. Gurley

(Windsor)

Total Taxable Property:

Land: 3906¼ a. - $168,666

Town Lots: 72 5/8 - $53,150

Slaves: 945 - $292,290

Interest received or due: $122,257

Bank dividends received or due: $3,018

Bank Officers: $4,250

Physicians: $4,000

Gold Watches: $2,620

Silver Watches: $496

Pianos: 11

Plate and Jewelry: $1,747

Pleasure Vehicles: $4,620

Household Furniture: $6,921

Lawyers: $1,000

State and County Officers: $1,500

Value of other property: $1,250

Total Value: $667,785

Total number of white voters: 54

Total number of colored voters: 2

Total number of people listed: 164

SALMON CREEK DISTRICT

BAYLEY, ANN, MRS.

    Land: Maple Swamp 124 a. ($500).

BAYLEY, MARTHA MRS.

    Land: Mill Swamp 150 a. ($450); Slaves: 1 ($800); Interest: ($258); Pleasure Vehicles: 1 ($75).

BAYLEY, THOMAS   voter

    Land: Blk. Walnut Swamp 138 a. ($621); Slaves: 7 ($2300); Interest: ($500).

BOSWELL, WM. heirs (by Jas. H. W. Smith)

    Land: Mill Swamp 65 a. ($130).

BOWEN, GEORGE   voter

    Land: Ducking Run 150 a. ($300).

BOWEN, HENRY   voter

    Land: Piney Woods 82 a. ($164).

BOWEN, HUMPHREY H.   voter

    Land: Piney Woods 82 a. ($123).

BOWEN, HOTIVID E.   voter

    Land: Piney Woods 100 a. ($200).

BOWEN, JESSE

    Land: Near Merry Hill 100 a. ($350); Interest: ($100).

BOWEN, JESSE T.   voter

    Land: Piney Woods 60 a. ($90).

(Salmon Creek)

BOWEN, JOSHUA

    Land: Piney Woods 50 a. ($75).

BOWEN, WILLIAM H.   voter

    Land: Bucklesbury 21 a. ($63).

BOWEN, WILLIAM R.   voter

    Land: Piney Woods 188 a. ($288).

BRETT, JAMES M.   voter

    Land: Cashoke 17 a. ($51).

BROWN, ELISHA   voter

    Land: Merry Hill 26 a. ($78).

BUM, JOHN A. heirs

    Interest: ($2383).

BUTTERTON, JAMES

    Land: Cashoke 200 a. ($794); Interest: ($175); Pleasure Vehicles: 1; ($75).

CAPEHART, CULLEN

    Land: Blk. Walnut Sound and Bucklesbury 8281 a. ($73558); Slaves: 258 ($77400); Interest: ($25533); Silver Watches: ($20); Piano: 1; Pleasure Vehicles: 1 ($50), 1 ($250); Household Furniture: ($800).

CAPEHART, GEORGE W.

    Land: Sound and Bucklesbury 1301 a. ($11580); Slaves: 39 ($13309); Gold Watches: 1 ($50); Pianos: 1 ; Pleasure Vehicles: 1 ($400); Household Furniture: ($400).

(Salmon Creek)

CAPEHART, TRISTRUMS heirs

    Land: Salmon Creek and Piney Woods 100 a. ($60).

CAPEHART, WM. H.

    Land: Merry Hill 181 a. ($1100); Interest: ($2000); Pleasure Vehicles: ($125).

CASTELLOW, TRISTRUM   voter

    Land: Bucklesbury 50 a. ($125).

DAVICE, JOSEPH O.   voter

DEMPSEY, JAMES

    Land: Mill Swamp 10 a. ($50).

DUNNING, WILLIAM

    Land: Salmon Creek 180 a. ($540).

FREEMAN, JAS. C.   voter

    Slaves: 12 ($5000); Silver Watches: ($20); Pleasure Vehicles: 1 ($50).

FREEMAN, RICH. P.

    Land: Salmon Creek and Wood Island 308 a. ($1800); Slaves: 13 ($3900); Interest: ($4050); Gold Watches: ($25); Pleasure Vehicles: 1 ($125), 1 ($175), 1 ($75); Household Furniture: ($50).

FREEMAN AND SUTTON

    Land: Near Nicholls and Road 100 a. ($300).

GILL, JOHN   voter

    Land: Piney Woods 161 a. ($402).

(Salmon Creek)

HARDIN, HARDY L. B.   voter

    Land: Bucklesbury 359 a. ($897).

HARDIN, LEVIS   voter

    Land: Bear Swamp and Roddett Track 890 a. ($2800); Slaves: 2 ($700).

HODDER, JAMES C.   voter

    Land: Cashoke 26 a. ($78).

HOLDER, WILLIAM A.   voter

    Silver Watches: ($15).

JOHNSTON, JOHN

    Land: Salmon Creek 175 a. ($150).

JOHNSTON, JOHN W.   voter

JONES, JAMES

    Land: Bucklesbury 52 a. ($156).

KEETER, CHARLES L.

    Land: Bucklesbury 181 a. ($490).

LANGDALE, GEORGE

    Land: Langdale Swamp 128 a. ($384); Slaves: 1 ($200).

LANGDALE, JOHN N.   voter

    Land: Bucklesbury 50 a. ($100); Silver Watches: ($10).

LEICESTER, JAMES H.   voter

    Land: Cashoke (no acreage or value listed).

(Salmon Creek)

LEICESTER, JONATHAN

    Land: Bucklesbury 67 a. ($197).

LEICESTER, WM. E.   voter

McGEE, JAMES

    Land: Hopewell Fishery 25 a. ($1000).

MITCHELL, GEORGE   voter

    Land: Bucklesbury 50 a. ($50).

MORESS, JOHN

    Land: Cashoke 21 a. ($100).

MORGAN, PETERS heirs

    Land: Cypress 210 a. ($735); Interest: ($175).

MOUNTAIN, P. H.

    Land: Cashoke 524 a. ($2358); Slaves: 14 ($5100); Pleasure Vehicles: 1 ($50).

MOUNTAIN, WM. E.   voter

NICHOLLS, JOHN heirs

    Land: Stoney Run 60 a. ($120).

NICHOLLS, JOSEPH B.   voter

    Land: Albemarle Sound 475 a. ($2137); Slaves: 7 ($1500); Interest: ($500); Pleasure Vehicles: 1 ($50).

NICHOLLS MARTHA E. estate

    Land: Cashoke 60 a. ($231); Interest: ($800).

ODER, RUBEN   voter

(Salmon Creek)

OWNLEY, MARY

    Interest: ($500).

PEARCE, RICHARDSON

    Land: Cashoke 430 a. ($2250); Slaves: 13 ($4010); Interest: ($250); Pleasure Vehicles: 1 ($50).

PETERSON, SUSAN A. estate

    Land: 800 a. ($2400); Slaves: 14 ($4475).

PHELPS, ABRAM   voter

PHELPS, ASA   voter

    Land: Cashoke 468 a. ($1800); Interest: ($1000); Silver Watches: ($10); Cattle: 4 ($24).

PHELPS, CHARLES   voter

    Land: Bucklesbury 100 a. ($250).

PHELPS, GEORGE   voter

    Land: Cashoke 17 a. ($34).

PHELPS, JAMES   voter

    Land: Bucklesbury 148 a. ($444); Slaves: 3 ($1400); Silver Watches: ($15); Piano: 1; Pleasure Vehicles: 1 ($50).

PHELPS, JOHN D.

    Land: Cashoke 105 a. ($525); Slaves: 9 ($2700); Pleasure Vehicles: 1 ($600).

PHELPS JOSEPH   voter

    Land: Cypress Swamp 160 a. ($400).

(Salmon Creek)

PHELPS, MICAJAH

    Land: Cashoke 111 a. ($222).

REDDITT, H. M. MRS.

    Land: Cashoke 1000 a. ($6000); Slaves: 7 ($2500).

RHODES, JONATHAN J.

    Land: Blk. Walnut Swamp 340 a. ($1700).

ROUNTREE, JACKSON   voter

    Slaves: 2 ($1300); Interest: ($1673); Gold Watches: ($30); Pleasure Vehicles: 1 ($50).

SHAW, JAMES   voter

    Land: Cashoke 79 a. ($316).

SHAW, SAMUEL

    Land: Cashoke 25 a. ($75).

SHIELDS, ROBT, A., DR.   voter

    Gold Watches: ($35); Silver Watches: ($20); Pleasure Vehicles: 1 ($75); Household Furniture: ($50).

SMITH, JAMES W.   voter

    Interest: ($400); Pleasure Vehicles: 1 ($50).

SMITHWICK, WILLIAM   voter

    Land: Cashoke 215 a. ($752); Slaves: 1 ($470); Interest: ($1673); Pleasure Vehicles: 1 ($70); (Also paid for one free colored poll).

SUTTON, WM. T.

    Land: Salmon Creek and Sound 3600 a. ($35625); Slaves: 192 ($50880); Gold Watches: ($50); Piano: 1; Pleasure Vehicles: 1 ($100); Household Furniture: ($500).

(Salmon Creek)

THOMPSON, JAMES R.   voter

    Land: Bucklesbury 70 a. ($210).

VALENTINE, JOHN B.   voter

    Land: Lawrence Mill 200 a. ($500).

WEBB, JOHN N.

    Land: Nicholls and Road 506 a. ($2000); Slaves: 17 ($4625); Pleasure Vehicles: 1 ($75); Household Furniture: ($50).

WEBB, JOHN N. JUNIOR   voter

    Slaves: 7 ($2505).

WEBB, THOS. B. heirs

    Land: Merry Hill 23 a. ($46).

WHITE, DORCEY   voter

    Slaves: 1 ($700).

WHITE, HEZEKIA   voter

    Land: Ducking Run 132 a. ($366).

WHITE, LODAWICK   voter

    Land: Piney Woods 80 a. ($110); Slaves: 3 ($800); Silver Watches: ($10).

WHITE, SOPHIE and AZEY

    Slaves: 2 ($900).

WHITE, ZACK   voter

    Land: Piney Woods 401 a. ($1041); Silver Watches: ($12).

(Salmon Creek)

WILLIFORD, JOSEPH W.

    Slaves: 2 ($940).

Persons and Property Not Listed

ARMISTEAD, THOS. (listed later)

    Land: Lower Rock Point and Kelly Hawk 9 a. ($4000).

CAPEHART, B. A. (listed later)   voter

    Land: Fishery on Roanoke 100 a. ($800); Slaves: 19 (no value listed); Interest: ($896); Bank Dividends: ($823); Gold Watches: 1 ($125); Plate and Jewelry ($800); Pleasure Vehicles: ($125).

COFFIELD, GEORGE   voter

CULLPHER, HENRY (listed later)

    Land: 2 a. ($10).

DAVICE, JONATHAN T.   voter

GARRABALDI, ANDREW CAPT. (listed later)

    Land: Middle River 5½ a. ($300).

MARDRE, THOS. A. (listed later)   voter

    Land: Merry Hill and Piney Woods 170 a. ($450).

NICHOLLS, JOHN

PHELPS, HENY (listed later)

    Land: Cashoke 17 a. ($35).

PIERCE, HEMY   voter

RAZOR, GILBERT D.   voter

(Salmon Creek)

SHORT AND BATEMAN   (listed later)

    Land: 600 a. ($100).

WATTERS, HARDY H.   (listed later)

    Land: Rose Bay Fishery 10 a. ($1000).

WHITE, HEMY   (listed later)

    Land: Cypress Swamp 425 a. ($850); Slaves: 5 ($1900).

WILLIS, ELISHA H.   (listed later)

    Land: Upper Rock Point 5 a. ($1500).

Total Taxable Property:

Land: 25930½ a. - $171,886

Slaves: 651 ; $190,314

Interest recieved or due: $42,866

Bank dividends recieved or due: $823

Gold Watches: $315

Silver Watches: $132

Pianos: 4

Plate and Jewelry: $800

Pleasure Vehicles: 22 - $2305

Household Furniture: $1850

Cattle: 4 - $24

Total Value: $411,315

Total number of colored voters: 1

Total number of white voters: 49

SALMON CREEK DISTRICT MILITARY ROLL

Bayley, Thos.
Bowen, Alpheus
Bowen, Fredrick C.
Bowen, George
Bowen, H. H.
Bowen, Henry
Bowen, Hotivid E.
Bowen, James L.
Bowen, Jesse T.
Bowen, Marcus
Bowen, Thomas E.
Bowen, William H.
Brett, James M.
Butler, Cader
Butterton, James H.
Byrum, John
Cobb, George W.
Cobb, William
Coffeild, Davie J.
Coffield, George
Corbett, John
Davice, Jonathan T.
Davice, Joseph O.
Francis, James H.
Freeman, James C.
Gregory, John T.
Gregory, Lemuel
Gregory, William
Hader, James O.
Harden, Hardy L. B.
Holder, William A.
Johnston, John W.

Langdale, John N.
Lawrence, Baker
Leicester, James H.
Leicester, Wm. E.
Mardre, John W.
Mardre, Thos. A.
Mountain, William E.
Oder, Ruben
Phelps, Abram
Phelps, Asa
Phelps, Charles
Phelps, James Jr.
Phelps, John W.
Phelps, John W.
Phelps, Joseph
Phelps, Leonedus H.
Phelps, William T.
Pierce, Henry
Rayzor, Gilford
Rountree, Jackson
Shaw, James
Sutton, John
Suttun, Stark A.
Thompson, James R.
Webb, John N.
White, Dorsey
White, Hezekiah
White, Joseph W.
White, Zack
Williford, James
Williford, Joseph N.

"I solemnly swear that I have diligently inquired and have no just reason to believe that there is any propity or other subject of taxation in my District not entered and valued (where the same is required to be valued) in the above list and the foregoing valuation in my judgement and belief is a fact actual value thereof in cash and that in assessing the same I have endeavored to do Equal justice to the publick and to individuals concerned, so help me God--"

                        R. Pearce

TRAP DISTRICT

ALSTON, JAMES   voter

    Land: 114 a. ($450); Slaves: 2 ($525).

AMBERS, BRITTON   voter

    Land: 120 a. ($500); Slaves: 2 ($700).

BASS, AUGUSTUS SEN.

    Land: 492 a. ($414).

BASS, AUGUSTUS JUN.   voter

    Slaves: 9 ($2,185); Silver Watch ($8).

BIRDS, ELIZA

    Land: 51 a. ($150).

BRITTON, JOHN S.   voter

    Land : 1,300 a. ($5,000); Slaves: 33 ($8,900); Silver Watches ($25); Pleasure Vehicles ($115).

BROWN, ANDREW J.   voter

BROWN, ISAAC

    Land: 80 a. ($250).

BURRUS, JAMES

    Land: 5 a. ($20).

BYRUM, HENRY H.

    Land: 160 a. ($500).

COFFIELD, ALFRED   heirs   (see Ruffin, M. Whites).

(Trap)

EARLY, ANDREW J.

    Land: 100 a. ($200); Slaves: 3 ($800).

EASON, MARY

    Land: 1,000 a. ($1,800).

FREEMAN, CYNTHA

    Land: 33 a. ($100).

FREEMAN, HOWELL for (Emily Thomas)

    Land: 155 a. ($300).

FREEMAN, ISAAC P.

    Land: 1704 a. ($4,700); Slaves: 65 ($16,475); Piano: ($50); Pleasure Vehicle: ($200); Household & Kitchen Furniture: ($150).

    do for David Watford - voter - Land; 409 a. ($1,540); Slaves: 10 ($2,500); Interest: ($2,564); Silver Watch: ($40); Pleasure vehicle: ($75).

FREEMAN, JOHN   voter

    Land: 58 a. ($80).

FREEMAN, JOHN B.

    Land: 1455 a. ($2,650); Slaves: 31 ($8,600).

FREEMAN, JOSIAH

    Land: 69 a. ($200).

FREEMAN, MARTHA

    Land: 46 a. ($133).

FREEMAN, RIDDICK   voter

    Land: 100 a. ($300).

(Trap)

FREEMAN, WM. H.   voter
    Land: 155 a. ($750); Slaves: 3 ($550).

FREEMAN, WM. J.   voter
    Land: 185 a. ($300); Interest: ($1100); Silver Watch: ($10).

GARRETT, RICHARD   voter
    Land: 307 a. ($1000); Slaves: 5 ($1,275).

GREEN, JOHN A.   voter
    Land: 44 a. ($200).

GREEN, GEORGE N.
    Land: 34 a. ($200).

HOBBS, CHARLES C.   voter
    Silver Watch: ($15).

HOBBS, JOSEPH   voter
    Land: 68 a. ($350).

HOBBS, SILAS
    Land: 409 a. ($546).

HOLOMON, GEORGE D. (of Hertford Co.)
    Land: 120 a. ($150).

HOLOMON, JAMES D.   by Daniel V. Sessoms
    Land: 260 a. ($350).

(Trap)

HOLOMON, WHITMEL
    Land: 12 a. ($75).

LEE, ANDREW J.   voter
    Land: 180 a. ($360).

LEE, DAVID   voter
    Land: 190 a. ($800); Pleasure Vehicles: ($50).

MILLER, ELISHA SEN.
    Land: 50 a. ($200).

MILLER, ELISHA JUN.   voter
    Land: 17 a. ($75).

MILLER, JESSE   voter

MILLER, LEVY   (Joseph J. Perry, Trustee)
    Land: 174 a. ($300).

MILLER, RIDDICK
    Land: 218 a. ($600); Pleasure Vehicles: ($50).

MILLER, WILLIAM
    Land: 88 a. ($400).

MITCHELLS, AARON
    Land: 53 a. ($200).

(Trap)

MITCHELLS, JERMIAH

    Land: 112 a. ($600); Slaves: 2 ($800).

MITCHELLS, WM. L.   voter

    Land: 30 a. ($100).

MORRISS, ALPHEUS   voter

MORRISS, GRANVILL G.   (see Harriet Morriss).

MORRISS, HARRIET

    Land: 720 a. ($3500); Slaves: 2 ($500).

    do for Granvill G. Morriss   Slaves: 3 ($475); Pleasure Vehicles: ($50).

NERNY, WM. JUN.   voter

    Land: 10 a. ($14).

NOWELL, ALPHEUS   voter

    Land: 208 a.($7 ; Slaves: 5 ($1025); Silver Watches: ($10); Pleasure Vehicles: ($50).

OUTLAW, FREEMAN

    Land: 200 a. ($400).

PEARCE, SAMUEL M.   voter

    Land: 53 a. ($350); Interest: ($50).

PERRY, JOHN

    Land: 825 a. ($3300); Slaves: 8 ($2025); Interest: ($2200); Pleasure Vehicles: ($50); Household & Kitchen Furniture: ($50).

(Trap)

    Do for his children   Slaves: 4 ($1450); Interest: ($900).

    Do for Mary A. Perry   Interest: ($1661).

    Do for Sarah J. Perry   Interest: ($1850).

    Do for Nancy Perry   Interest: ($1905).

    Do for Martha Perry   Interest: ($1970).

    Do for Wm. W. Perry   Interest: ($1805).

    Do for John Perry   Interest: ($2070).

    Do for minor heirs of Wm. Perry   Slaves: 11 ($2950).

    Do for Wm. D. Perry   Land: 113 a. ($266).

    Do for Thomas Perry   Land: 183 a. ($700); Slaves: 2 ($675); Interest: ($585).

    Do for Martin V. B. Perry   Land: 100 a. ($300); Interest: ($3024).

PERRY, JOHN W.   voter

    Land: 280 a. ($1010); Slaves: 5 ($1125); Silver Watches: ($20); Pleasure Vehicles: ($100).

    Do for James M. Perry   Land: 150 a. ($610); Slaves: 4 ($700); Pleasure Vehicles: ($100).

PERRY, JOS. S.   voter

    Pleasure Vehicles: ($100).

PERRY, JOSEPH J.   voter

    Land: 600 a. ($1737); Slaves: 15 ($3800); Interest: ($600); Silver Watches: ($8); Pleasure Vehicles: ($100).

PERRY, SUSAN MRS.

    Slaves: 6 ($825).

(Trap)

RAYNER, JOHN A.   voter

    Slaves: 4 ($900).

    Do for Wm. Rayner Estate   Land: 425 a. ($1300); Slaves: 22 ($5375); Pleasure Vehicles: ($50).

RAYNER, MARCUS J.   voter

RAYNER, WM. ESTATE   (see John A. Rayner)

ROBBINS, AUGUSTUS   free colored voter

    Land: 50 a. ($100).

ROBBINS, NOAH

    Land: 43 a. ($86).

ROBBINS, PARKER   free colored voter

    Land: 50 a. ($100); Interest: ($250).

RUFFIN, JOSEPH B.   voter

SESSOMS, A. B.   (see Wm. H. Tayloe).

SESSOMS, AM.   (see Wm. H. Tayloe).

SESSOMS, AMGRID W. Heirs   (see Wm. H. Tayloe).

SESSOMS, ASSAN   voter

    Land: 405 a. ($986); Slaves: 11 ($2050).

SESSOMS, JOS. L.   Estate

    (Daniel V. Sessoms, Administratin)   Collateral Descents, Devises, and Bequests   ($694).

(Trap)

SESSOMS, JOSEPH W.   voter

    Land: 265 a. ($1000); Slaves: 11 ($2675); Physician: ($700); Gold Watches: ($75); Pleasure Vehicles: ($60).

SESSOMS, MILLY F.   Estate

    (Daniel V. Sessoms, Administratin) Collateral Descents, Devises, and Bequests: ($736).

TAYLOE, WM. H.   voter

    Land: 1364 a. ($4,000); Slaves: 48 ($13,000); Interest: ($600); Stud Horses and Jacks: 8; Silver Watches: ($15); Pleasure Vehicles: ($200); Household & Kitchen Furniture: ($50).

    Do for Am. Sessoms   Interest: ($185).

    Do for Amgrid W. Sessoms, Heirs   Land: 438 a. ($875); Slaves: 4 ($1750).

    Do for A. B. Sessoms   Interest: ($304).

THOMAS, EMILY   (see Howell Freeman).

WATFORD, DAVID   (see Isaac P. Freeman).

WHITES, NOAH   voter

    Land: 50 a. ($150).

    Do for Elizabeth White   Interest: ($464).

    Do for Milly White   Land: 84 a. ($247).

    Do for Jacob Whites Estate   Land: 169 a. ($503); Interest: ($1130).

WHITES, RUFFIN M.   voter

    Land: 700 a. ($1850); Slaves: 11 ($2275); Interest: ($3849).

    Do for Alfred Coffield, Heirs   Land: 238 a. ($617); Slaves: 13 ($3425); Interest: ($784).

(Trap)

WHITES, WM. W.   voter

    Land: 50 a. ($50); Gold Watches: ($35).

WILLIAM, JOHN F.

    Land: 141 a. ($600).

    Do for Mrs. Treasy White   Slaves: 4 ($1100).

WILLIAMS, BENGAMIN B.   voter

    Land: 83 a. ($350); Silver Watches: ($15).

    Do for Heirs of Jos. N. White   Land: 230 a. ($576); Slaves: 4 ($1700).

    Do Trustee for Wm. Williams   Land: 248 a. ($625); Slaves: 1 ($450).

TRAP DISTRICT MILITARY ROLL

Alston, James (vol.)
Ambers, Britton
Baker, Joseph (vol.)
Baker, Richard R.
Bass, Augustus
Britton, Daniel W. (vol.)
Britton, John L.
Brown, Andrew J.
Brown, Jacob (vol.)
Brown, W^m. H. (vol.)
Byrum, Henry H.
Byrum, James H. (vol.)
Byrum, Joseph O. (vol.)
Byrum, W^m. J. (vol.)
Early, Andrew J. (vol.)
Freeman, Howell (vol.)
Freeman, Jacob (vol.)
Freeman, James (vol.)
Freeman, John
Freeman, Josiah (vol.)
Freeman, Riddick N. (drafted)
Freeman, Romolus J. (vol.)
Freeman, Thomas H. (vol.)
Freeman, W^m. H. (drafted)
Freeman, W^m. J.
Garrett, Richard
Green, George N. (vol.)
Green, John A.
Harrell, David (vol.)
Harrell, George B. (vol.)
Hobbs, Charles C.
Hobbs, Charlton (vol.)
Hobbs, Henry A. (vol.)
Hobbs, Jos.
Holoman, James D. (vol.)

Jinkens, Winbon (vol.)
Lee, Andrew J.
Lee, David (vol.)
Miller, Charles (vol.)
Miller, Elisha
Miller, Henderson (vol.)
Miller, Jesse
Miller, Levy (vol.)
Mitchell, Thomas (vol.)
Mitchell, W^m. L.
Mizell, Henry C. (vol.)
Morriss, Alpjeus
Morriss, Granville G. (vol.)
Nerny, John (vol.)
Nerny, W^m. Sen.
Nerny, W^m. Jun.
Nowell, Alpheus (drafted)
Pearce, Samuel M. (capt.)
Perry, James M. (vol.)
Perry, John W.
Perry, Jos. J.
Perry, Jos. S. (drafted)
Perry, Thomas (vol.)
Perry, W^m. D. (vol.)
Perry, W^m. W. (vol.)
Rayner, John A.
Rayner, Marcus J.
Ruffin, Joseph B. (drafted)
Sessoms, Assan
Tayloe, W^m. H.
Trumble, John (vol.)
White, Noah A.
White, W^m. H. (drafted)
Williams, John F. (vol.)

" I solemnly swear that I have diligently inquired and have no just reason to believe that there is any property or other subjects of taxation in my district not intered and valued (where the same is required to be valued) in the above list, and the foregoing valuation, in my judgement and belief, is the fair, actual value thereof in cash; and that in assessing the same, I have endeavered to do equal Justice to the public and to the individuals concerned; so help me God."
       W^m. H. Tayloe List taxes

(Trap)

Total Taxable Property:

Land: 102,548 a.- $107,590

Slaves: 363 - $93,560

Interest received or due: $29,850

Silver Watches: $166

Gold Watches: $110

Piano: $50

Pleasure Vehicles: $1350

Household & Kitchen Furniture: $250

Physicians: $700

Collateral Descents, Devises, and Bequests: $1430

Stud Horses and Jacks: 8

Total Value: $235,056

Total number of white voters: 36

Total number of colored voters: 2

Total people listed: 88

INDIAN WOODS DISTRICT

ALSTON, W. SALLEY

    Slaves: 7 ($2700); Interest: ($90).

ASHBURN, MARY

    Land: Residence 1250 a. ($5000); Slaves: 21 ($5250); Interest: ($2500).

ASKEW, THOS. R.   voter

    Land: Cahsie Neck 612 a. ($9000); Slaves: 24 ($7200); Pleasure Vehicles: ($100).

ASKEW, W. L.   voter

    Land: 210 a. ($2100); Slaves: 6 ($1800); Silver Watches: ($20).

BOND, JAMES   voter

    Land: Residence 700 a. ($7000), 1800 a. ($2300), town lots 2 ($1975); Slaves: 54 ($1700); Interest: ($15650); Gold Watches: ($150); Plate and Jewelry: ($40); PleasureVehicles: ($350); Household Furniture: ($150).

BOND, LEWIS   voter

    Land: Residence 1000 a. ($12000), Roquist 1000 a. ($2000), Piney Woods 20 a. ($13); Slaves: 50 ($5000); Gold Watches: ($100); Pleasure Vehicles: ($150); Household Furniture: ($150).

BOND, LEWIS T.   voter

    Land: Residence 1000 a. ($1200), Pocsin 60 a. ($180); Slaves: 76 ($24300); Gold Watches: ($50); Pianos: 1; Plate and Jewelry: ($160); Pleasure Vehicles: ($400); Household Furniture: ($300).

BOND, MARY M. AND WILLIAM

    Land: Residence 180 a. ($1700), Pollocks 1400 a. ($1400), Cedar Landing 1000 a. ($8000); Slaves: 95 ($26200); Interest: ($24045).

(Indian Woods)

BUTLAR, JNO. T.   voter

BUTLAR, KENNITH   voter
    Land: 180 a. ($2000).

BUTLAR, LOUIZA
    Land: 1520 a. ($1200); Slaves: 8 ($2000).

CARTER, SALLIE, MRS.
    Slaves: 16 ($5700); Interest: ($2250).

CLARY, E. B., MRS.
    Slaves: 5 ($1750).

COGGIN, WILL G.   voter
    Note Shavers: ($30).

COLLINS, JAMES
    Land: Residence 400 a. ($1200).

CRAIG, A. (Jno. P. Rascoe Guardian)
    Slaves: 10 ($2400); Interest: ($4400).

DAVIS, AARON
    Land: 50 a. ($125); Slaves: 1 ($25).

DAVIS, MANNIA
    Land: 2 0 a. ($20).

DAVIS, NAZIRUTH   voter

(Indian Woods)

DEWES, JON. R.   voter

    Land: Pir^v Woods 107 a. ($107), 422 a. ($1200); Slaves: 16 ($5000).

FERGUSON, JOHN   voter

    Land: Broad Branch 130 a. ($2000), Slade 160 a. ($1000), town lot 1 ($1200); Slaves: 24 ($9000); Gold Watches: ($50).

GILLIAM, FRANK

    Land: Indian Woods 312 a. ($3700); Slaves: 15 ($5000); Interest: ($6800).

GILLIAM, JNO. B.   voter

GILLIAM, THOMAS   voter

    Land: Indian Woods 312 a. ($3700); Slaves: 29 ($9280); Gold Watches: ($38); Plate and Jewelry: ($60); Pleasure Vehicles: ($50).

GILLIAM, WILLIE J.

    Land: Cashie Neck 1250 a. ($15000), Residence 1800 a. ($7000); Slaves: 81 ($25300); Gold Watches: ($50); Plate and Jewelry: ($50). Pleasure Vehicles: ($250); Household Furniture: ($320).

HAMBLEIR, WILLIE MIS

    Land: Indian Woods Residence 1800 a. ($12000); Slaves: 26 ($9100); Interest: ($3000); Gold Watches: ($60); Piano: 1; Plate and Jewelry: ($200); Pleasure Vehicles: ($100); Household Furniture: ($600).

HECKSTAL, JAMES   voter

    Land: Cashie Neck Residence 283 a. ($1300); Slaves: 14 ($3450).

HECKSTALL, THOS. J.

    Land: Durgun District 325 a. ($1038), Residence 700 a. ($2500); Slaves: 16 ($4800); Interest: ($1000); Pleasure Vehicles: ($100).

(Indian Woods)

HECKSTALL, W. H. heirs

    Interest: ($762).

HOLADY, WM.   voter

HYMAN, JOEL   voter

    (Also paid for one free colored poll).

HYMAN, WILLIAM

    Land: Cashie Neck Residence 612 a. ($5000); Slaves: 15 ($4500); Ferries Total Recieved: ($225); Silver Watches: ($20); Pleasure Vehicles: ($150).

JACOCKS, JESSIE   voter

    Land: Hope 1800 a. ($12000); Slaves: 23 ($9200); Gold Watches: ($125); Pianos: 1; Plate and Jewelry: ($70); Pleasure Vehicles: ($300); Household Furniture: ($350).

JORDAN, JOSEPH

    Land: Residence 600 a. ($7200), Rhodes Place 275 a. ($1375), Quonine 200 a. ($2500), Roanoke Swamp 700 a. ($500); Slaves: 41 ($13250); Gold Watches: ($50); Pleasure Vehicles: ($50).

LAWRENCE, WILL estate

    Land: Roquist 250 a. ($500); Slaves: 7 ($2300).

MEBANE, A. W.   voter

    Slaves: 34 ($10200); Interest: ($33150); Gold Watches: ($100).

MILLER, F. C.   voter

    Land: Residence 600 a. ($7200), Folk Tract 500 a. ($5000), Roquist 300 a. ($2000), Brimage Track 760 a. ($1500); Slaves: 69 ($21000); Interest: ($4275); Gold Watches: ($80); Plate and Jewelry: ($35); Pleasure Vehicles: ($450); Household Furniture: ($200).

(Indian Woods)

MINTON, THS. and ELLA infant (Tho. Heckstall guardian)
   Interest: ($6320).

MITCHELL, JON. S.
   Land: Indian Woods 312 a. ($3700); Slaves: 14 ($4750).

MIZILLS, ISAAC
   Land: 175 a. ($650); Silver Watches: ($10).

MIZILLS, JON. J.   voter
   Land: 400 a. ($1000).

MOORE, SARAH A.
   Land: Roanoke Swamp 100 a. ($650).

MORING, WILLIAM (see also Mrs. Jno. Pool)
   Land: Residence 4840 a. ($40,000), Bonds Land 2604 a. ($18,000); Slaves: 144 ($43,200); Interest: ($3610); Bank Dividends: ($715); Stud Horses and Jacks: ($5); Gold Watches: ($40); Plate and Jewelry: ($25); Pleasure Vehicles: ($80); Household Furniture: ($200).

OUTLAW, D. C.
   Slaves: 9 ($2700).

OUTLAW, EDW. N.
   Slaves: 10 ($2800); Silver Watches: ($10).

PENNOYER, SYLVESTER
   Silver Watches: ($15).

POOL, JNO. MRS. (Will Moring and trustee)
   Land: 920 a. ($16,600); Slaves: 35 ($10,500).

(Indian Woods)

PRICE, EBINEZAR   voter

    Land: 100 a. ($500).

PRICE, JOHN

    Land: 316 a. ($400); Slaves: 3 ($800); Pleasure Vehicles: ($50).

PUGH, WILL. A.   voter

    Land: Roanoke River 4471 a. ($3900); Slaves: 72 ($25,200); Stud Horses and Jacks: 6; Gold Watches: ($125); Pianos 1; Plate and Jewelry: ($150); Pleasure Vehicles: ($100); Household Furniture: ($1000).

RANGE, WILLIAM

    Land: 33 a. ($165).

RASCOE, JON. P.

    Land: Residence 630 a. ($4500), Indian Wodds 918 a. ($8000), town lots 2 ($2500); Slaves: 90 ($25,000); Interest: ($48,000); Bank Dividends: ($650); Silver Watches: ($25); Piano: 1; Plate and Jewelry: ($45); Pleasure Vehicles: ($225); Household Furniture: ($250); (also paid for one free colored poll).

RASCOE, PETER   voter

    Gold Watches: ($120).

RIGSBY, WILLIAM   voter

SKILES, JNO.   voter

SMALLWOOD, J. P.   voter

    Land: Indian Woods 2200 a. ($22,000); Slaves: 90 ($30,000); Bank Dividends: ($520); Gold Watches: ($100); Piano: 1; Plate and Jewelry: ($100); Pleasure Vehicles: ($300); Household Furniture: ($600).

(Indian Woods)

SMALLWOOD, M. W.

    Interest: ($6593).

SPELLER, JAS. J.   voter

    Gold Watches: ($125).

SPIVEY, MARGT T., MIS

    Land: Residence 750 a. ($4000); Slaves: 16 ($4800); Interest: ($6900); Gold Watches: ($75); Plate and Jewelry: ($50); Household Furniture: ($200).

STEVE, WM.   voter

SWAIN, LAURA, MISS

    Land: Cashie Neck 200 a. ($2000); Slaves: 7 ($2300); Interest: ($2500).

SWAIN, WHIT   voter

    Land: Cashie Neck 360 a. ($4000); Slaves: 9 ($3600); Gold Watches: ($150); Pleasure Vehicles: ($125).

SWAIN, WHIT R.   voter

    Land: Cashie Neck 1990 a. ($15000); Slaves: 85 ($27500); Gold Watches: ($75); Pianos: 1; Plate and Jewelry: ($75); Pleasure Vehicles: ($175); Household Furniture: ($800).

WARD, JAMES H. (see W. H. White)   voter

    Land: 200 a. ($4850); Slaves: 22 ($6600); Pianos: 1; Pleasure Vehicles: ($352).

WARD, WILL T.

    Land: 200 a. ($500); Slaves: 9 ($3000); Interest: ($800); (also paid for one free colored poll).

(Indian Woods)

WASTON, THOS. C.

    Land: 780 a. ($3120); Slaves: 46 ($14700); Bank Dividends: ($139) Bank of North Carolina; Gold Watches: ($40); Pianos: 1; Plate and Jewelry: ($125); Pleasure Vehicles: ($150); Household Furniture: ($500).

WHITE, HARRISON

    Land: 150 a. ($150).

WHITE, W. H. (listed by J. H. Ward)

    Slaves: 11 ($4125); Pleasure Vehicles: ($125).

WILLIAMS, JOHN   voter

    Interest: ($500); Pleasure Vehicles: ($50).

Total Taxable Property

Land: 49,132 - $353,036

Town Lots: 5 - $5,675

Slaves: 1,458 - $456,980

Interest received or due: $179,565

Bank Dividends received or due: $2,024

Ferry Receipts: $225

Gold Watches: $1,703

Silver Watches: $100

Pianos: 9

Plate and Jewelry: $1,185

Note Shavers: $30

Stud Horses and Jacks: 11

Pleasure Vehicles: $4,180

Household Furniture: $5,270

(Indian Woods)

Total Value: $1,009,943

Total number of white voters: 33

Total number of colored voters: 3

Total people listed: 69

"I solemnly swear that I have diligently inquired and have no just reason to belive that there is any property in other subjects of taxation in my district not entered and valued * (when the land is required to be valued) in the above list; and the foregoing valuation in my judgement and belief, is the fair actual value therof in cash; and that assessing the same I have ordained to do equal justice to the public and to the individuals concern: so help me God.

         Tho. C. Watson

sworn and subscribed before me
  W. R. Gurly C. R.

*except the property of the persons returned on seperate paper here with as not listing.

SNAKEBITE DISTRICT

ANDERS, ABNER

    Land: 291 a. ($500); Pleasure Vehicles: ($250); Household Furniture: ($300).

ASKEW, GEORGE O. estate

    Land: 1081 a. ($5000); Slaves: 30 ($12000); Interest: ($8076).

AUSTIN, URIAH   voter

    Land: 40 a. ($106).

BAZEMORE, ALDEN   voter

    Land: 314 a. ($800); Slaves: 6 ($1600); Interest: ($1200); Pleasure Vehicles: ($75).

BAZEMORE, CULLEN H. (see Sharrock, Whitmel G.)

BAZEMORE, DAVID (see Sharrock, Whitmel G.)

BAZEMORE, EDWARD   voter

    Land: 369 a. ($1350); Slaves: 4 ($1200).

BAZEMORE, HENRY   voter

    Land: 150 a. ($550); Slaves: 3 ($1500); Interest: ($169).

BAZEMORE, JAMES N.

    Land: 430 a. ($600); Slaves: 1 (not given).

BAZEMORE, JESSE

    Land: 501 a. ($2100); Slaves: 9 ($2700).

BAZEMORE, JOHN T. (see Sharrock, Whitmel G.)

(Snakebite)

BAZEMORE, KENNETH   voter

    Land: 265 a. ($475).

BAZEMORE, PERMILIA (see Sharrock, Whitmel G.)

BAZEMORE, REDIN

    Land: 250 a. ($250); Slaves: 18 ($7200); Interest: ($152).

BAZEMORE, STEPHEN

    Land: 850 a. ($3100); Slaves: 14 ($4800); Pleasure Vehicles:
    ($50); Household Furniture: ($25).

BRIDGES, ROBERT M.   voter

    Land: 350 a. ($600); Slaves: 8 ($2400); Interest: ($600);
    Gold Watches: ($40).

BROGDON, HENRY A.   voter

BUNCH, JEREMIAH JUN.   voter

    Land: 881 a. ($3000); Slaves: 21 ($6300); Gold Watches:
    ($30); Pleasure Vehicles: ($130); Household Furniture: ($65).

BUNCH, JESSE

    Land: 76 a. ($200).

BUNCH, JESSE H.   voter

    Land: 200 a. ($425); Silver Watches: ($5).

BUNCH, NEHEMIAH J.   voter

    Land: 391 a. ($700); Interest: ($666); Gold Watches: ($25);
    Pleasure Vehicles: ($75).

BUNCH, TEMPERANCE

    Land: 545 a. ($1100); Slaves: 12 ($4500).

(Snakebite)

BUNCH, WILLIAM H.

    Land: 734 a. ($3500); Slaves: 5 ($2100); Silver Watches: ($25); Pleasure Vehicles: ($100); Household Furniture: ($25).

BURDEN, JAMES   voter

    Land: 600 a. ($4000); Slaves: 4 ($950); Gold Watches: ($50); Pleasure Vehicles: ($50).

BURDEN, JOHN L.   voter

    Land: 300 a. ($1800); Slaves: 8 ($3000); Pleasure Vehicles: ($75).

BURDEN, ZADOK J.   voter

    Land: 222 a. ($800); Slaves: 7 ($2000).

BUTLER, BENJAMIN

    Land: 87 a. ($175).

BUTLER, JACOB J.

    Land: 30 a. ($30).

BUTLER, JAMES   voter

    Land: 50 a. ($100).

BUTLER, JOHN T.   voter

    Land: 50 a. ($150).

BYRUM, JAMES

    Land: 68 a. ($100).

CASPER, ASA   voter

    Land: 100 a. ($125).

(Snakebite)

CASPER, CULLEN, SR.

    Land: 410 a. ($2500); Slaves: ($4700); Interest: ($358); Pleasure Vehicles: ($50); Household Furniture: ($25).

CASPER, CULLEN, JR.   voter

    Slaves: 2 ($750); Pleasure Vehicles: ($50).

CASPER, GEORGE M.   voter

    Land: 196 a. ($400).

CASPER, THOMAS, JR.

    Land: 200 a. ($1250); Slaves: 6 ($1700).

CASPER, WILLIAM, SR.

    Land: 1020 a. ($3000).

CHAPEL, WILLIAM L.

    Land: 150 a. ($500); Slaves: 4 ($1000); Interest: ($2000).

CHERRY, AARON

    Land: 590 a. ($1350); Slaves: 38 ($13000); Interest: ($12000).

CHERRY, JOSPH W.   voter

    Land: 100 a. ($300); Slaves: 1 ($500); Silver Watches: ($10).

CHERRY, THEOPHILUS

    Land: 2050 a. ($8300).

CHERRY, THOMAS

    Land: 549 a. ($2475); Slaves: 22 ($8700); Interest: ($2664).

CHERRY, WILLIAM J.

    Land: 450 a. ($1100); Slaves: 7 ($2400); Pleasure Vehicles: ($60).

(Snakebite)

CHERRY, DOCTOR'S HEIRS   (William J. Cherry guardian)

    Land: 467 a. ($1667); Slaves: 18 ($5400); Interest: ($5000).

COLLINS, WILLIAM   voter

    Land: 124 a. ($700).

COWAN, ROBERT A.   voter

    Land: 200 a. ($500); Slaves: 1 ($500); Pleasure Vehicles: ($50).

DAWSON, WILLIAM H.   voter

DRAKE, WILLIAM H.   voter

    Land: 126 a. ($225); Slaves: 1 ($200).

DUNNING, MARY

    Land: 109 a. ($150).

EVANS, DAVID D.   voter

    Silver Watches: ($10).

FREEMAN, GEORGE

    Land: 37 a. ($75).

GARDNER, JOHN

    Land: 60 a. ($100).

HARMON, CHARLES W.   (sta)

    Interest: ($2161).

HARMON, CHRISTIAN   (cont.)

(Snakebite)

    Land: 315 a. ($650).

HARMON, ELI   voter

    Land: 321 a. ($854); Slaves: 2 ($600).

HARMON, ENOCH   voter

    Land: 890 a. ($2000); Slaves: 3 ($750).

HARMON, RICHARD T.

    Land: 675 a. ($2000); Slaves: 19 ($5800); Interest: ($9293); Bank Dividends: ($130) in Bank of North Carolina.

HARMON, ROBT. M. M.   est (per Wm. H. Bunch guard.)

    Slaves: 6 ($2400); Interest: ($3330).

HARRELL, PENELOPY

    Land: 15 a. ($30).

HARRIS, JOHN

    Land: 100 a. ($100).

HOGGARD, RICHARD

    Land: 260 a. ($350); Slaves: 3 ($1000).

HOWARD, JAMES R.

    Land: 219 a. ($800).

HOWARD, JESSIE J.

    Land: 260 a. ($500); Slaves: 6 ($2000); Interest: ($300).

HOWARD, JOHN (cont.)

(Snakebite)

Land: 515 a. ($1000); Slaves: 9 ($2900); Interest: ($400).

HOWARD, JOSEPH   voter

Slaves: 1 ($500).

JERNIGAN, ALFRED   voter

Land: 80 a. ($100).

JERNIGAN, WILLIAM   voter

Land: 170 a. ($250).

MATTHEWS, JACOB

Land: 60 a. ($160).

MOORE, CALVIN   voter

Land: 409 a. ($500).

MORRIS, ALLEN

Land: 398 a. ($500).

MORRIS, ANDREW (not listed)

MORRIS, JOSEPH

Land: 100 a. ($150).

MYERS, LARNCE O.   voter

Land: 400 a. ($1100).

MYERS, RALPH D.   voter

Interest: ($375); Pleasure Vehicles: ($75).

7

(Snakebite)

MYERS, WILLIAM

    Land: 110 a. ($375); Slaves: 1 ($300).

MYERS, WILLIAM H.   voter

    Land: 156 a. ($375).

PARKER, BARBARA

    Slaves: 6 ($1700).

PARKER, WILLIAM G.

    Land: 850 a. ($5000); Slaves: 13 ($4200).

PEELLE, DREW   voter

    Land: 200 a. ($800); Slaves: 2 ($800); Pleasure Vehicles: ($75).

PEELLE, JAMES   voter

    Land: 48 a. ($125).

PEELLE, JARROT

    Land: 825 a. ($2000); Slaves: 9 ($2600).

PEELLE, SARAH

    Land: 277 a. ($850); Slaves: 4 ($800).

PRITCHARD, ALLEN

    Land: 900 a. ($1600); Slaves: 16 ($4800); Interest: ($200); Pleasure Vehicles: ($75); Household Furniture: ($25).

PRITCHARD, AMILLIA E.

    Interest: ($350).

(Snakebite)

PRITCHARD, CALVIN
    Interest: ($330).

PRITCHARD, ELIZABETH
    Interest: ($350).

PRITCHARD, ERVIN   voter

PRITCHARD, GEORGE W.
    Interest: ($450).

PRITCHARD, HUTSON
    Land: 236 a. ($500).

PRITCHARD, JAMES
    Land: 52 a. ($150); Interest: ($700).

PRITCHARD, LOUIZA
    Interest: ($350).

PRITCHARD, MARY B.
    Interest: ($350).

PRITCHARD, OUTLAW   voter
    Land: 175 a. ($400).

PRITCHARD, SARAH F.
    Interest: ($350).

PRITCHARD, WILLIAM   voter
    Land: 331 a. ($600); Slaves: 1 ($10).

(Snakebite)

PRUDEN, JACOB   voter

  Land: 1026 a. ($1875); Slaves: 1 ($500).

RAWLS, MOORE

  Land: 332 a. ($1000); Interest: ($1335); Silver Watches: ($40); Pleasure Vehicles: ($140); (also paid for one free colored poll).

RICE, DORSEY   voter

  Land: 175 a. ($350); Slaves: 3 ($1100); Pleasure Vehicles: ($50).

RICE, MARY

  Land: 50 a. ($100); Slaves: 2 ($600).

RICE, THOMAS T.   voter

  Land: 228 a. ($325); Slaves: 1 ($400); Interest: ($300).

SANDERS, ROBERT E.   voter

SHARROCK, WHITMEL G.

  Land: 1870 a. ($15000); Slaves: 41 ($15000); Interest: ($4000); Gold Watches: ($65); Pianos: 2; Pleasure Vehicles: ($300); Household Furniture: ($250).

  guardian for:

  Cullen H. Bazemore - Slaves: 2 ($1100); Interest: ($461).
  David Bazemore - Slaves: 4 ($800); Interest: ($529).
  John T. Bazemore - Slaves: 2 ($850); Interest: ($721).
  Permilia Bazemore - Slaves: 3 ($1400); Interest: ($529).

SIMMONS, SAMUEL W.

  Land: 155 a. ($1000); Slaves: 2 ($300).

SIMMONS, WILLIAM J.   voter

(Snakebite)

SLADE, NANCY

    Land: 50 a. ($200).

SPIVEY, WILLIAM

    Land: 950 a. ($5000); Slaves: 27 ($8800); Interest: ($3340);
    Pianos: 1; Pleasure Vehicles: ($200); Household Furniture: ($100).

TAYLOE, JAMES   voter

TAYLOE, RICHARD R.

    Land: 100 a. ($400).

TODD, LITTLETON J.

    Land: 345 a. ($1500); Slaves: 11 ($3000); Interest: ($541);
    Pleasure Vehicles: ($75).

VEAL, RICHARD J.

    Land: 1100 a. ($10000); Slaves: 28 ($7676); Interest: ($3500);
    Pianos: 1; Pleasure Vehicles: ($350); Household Furniture: ($200).

WESTON, MALACHI   voter

    Land: 388 a. ($1540); Interest: ($600).

WESTON, SUSAN

    Slaves: 3 ($1200); Pleasure Vehicles: ($100).

WILLIAMS, ELIZABETH

    Land: 260 a. ($500); Interest: ($300).

(Snakebite)

Persons and Property Not Listed

BAZEMORE, STARKY

BUNCH, CELIA

BUNCH, NEHEMIAH (in the army) (listed later)
    Land: 375 a. ($1200).

BUTLER, WORLEY (in the army) (listed later)
    Land: 30 a. ($100).

CASPER, KENNETH'S CHILDREN

CASPER, THOMAS, JR. (in the army) (listed later)
    Land: 300 a. ($572).

CHERRY, DOCTOR (land not listed)

CHERRY, SARAH A.

COOPER, NANCY (listed later)
    Land: 66 a. ($300).

COOPER, NORFLET

EASON, HARRIET (listed later)
    Land: 343 a. ($400).

FREEMAN, JOHN (listed later)
    Land: 300 a. ($600).

JERNIGAN, Wm. H. (in the army)

(Snakebite)

Persons and Property Not Listed

MITCHELL, GEORGE H. (listed later)

    Land: not given ($1000).

MORRIS, WILLIAM (in the army "in the woods") (listed later)

    Land: 100 a. ($200).

Total Taxable Property:

Land: 33,943 a. - $123,209

Slaves: 493 - $164,986

Interest received or due: $68,430

Bank dividends received or due: $130

Silver Watches: $90

Gold Watches: $210

Pianos: 4

Pleasure Vehicles: $2,455

Household Furniture: $950

Total Value: $360,460

Total number of white voters: 45

Total number of colored voters: 1

Total people listed: 128

HOTEL DISTRICT

BALLANCE, JAS. W.   voter

   Land: 600 a. ($7000).

BALLANCE, JOHN W. (by guardian)

   Slaves: 22 ($6600); Silver Watches: ($40); Pleasure Vehicles: ($140).

BARRETT, M. E. G.   voter

   Land: 484 a. ($2000); Slaves: 7 ($1880); Pleasure Vehicles: ($100);
   Household Furniture: ($100).

BAZEMORE ANN A.

   Slaves: 2 ($600); Interest: ($159).

BAZEMORE, JOS. P.   voter

   Land: 211 a. ($500); Slaves: 2 ($1000); Silver Watches: ($10).

BERNARD, L. A., DR.   voter

   Land: 3 a. ($500); Physician: ($2000); Gold Watches: ($50);
   Pleasure Vehicles: ($100).

BISHOP, M. P. (not given in)

BOND, GEORGE T. (by guardian)

   Slaves: 1 ($400).

BOND, WATSON J. LAVAGE

BOND, WM. T.   voter

   Land: 496 a. ($4000); Slaves: 11 ($3150); Gold Watches: ($50);
   Pleasure Vehicles: ($150); Household Furniture: ($150); (Also
   paid for one free colored poll).

(Hotel)

BOYKIN, L. M. est. (by M. E. G. Barrett)

    Interest: ($689).

BOYKIN, LOUISA L. (by M.E.G. Barrett)

    Interest: ($583).

BOYKIN, NANCY (by M. E. G. Barrett)

    Interest: ($637).

BROWN, ROBERT   voter

    Land: 5 a. ($300); Slaves: 1 ($200); Silver Watches: ($30); Pleasure Vehicles: ($100).

BRYAN, JOHN L.

    Land: acres not given ($2250).

BUNCH, REDDICK est. (by adms.)

    Land: 300 a. ($1200).

BUNCH, WM. D.   voter

    Silver Watches: ($25).

CARSON, ROBERT

    Land: Martin County 273 a. ($900).

CLARK, DAVID C.

    Land: 1000 a. ($15000); Slaves: 65 ($22000).

CLARK, GAVIN H.   voter

    Land: 1500 a. ($27500); Slaves: 85 ($25000); Gold Watches: ($65); Piano: 1; Plate and Jewelry: ($50); Pleasure Vehicles: ($200); Household Furniture: ($300).

(Hotel)

CLARK, GEORGE   voter
    Land: 200 a. ($2000); Slaves: 7 ($2100); Pleasure Vehicles: ($50).

CLARK, JOHN minor heirs (by E. Hancock)
    Land: 410 a. ($2500); Slaves: 12 ($3600); Interest: ($2230).

COT, THOMAS   voter
    Land: 365 a. ($1240); Pleasure Vehicles: ($75).

CRICKLON, JOHN, DR.   voter
    Gold Watches: ($75).

DAVIS, CHARLES J.

DAVIS, JAMES L. D.   voter

DAVIS, T. B.   voter
    Interest: ($245); Silver Watches: ($20).

DEVREUX, JOHN

DICKINS, WM. C.   voter
    Interest: ($424); Silver Watches: ($30); Pleasure Vehicles: ($50).

EARLY, JAK (Mrs. Martha Williford, overseer)   voter
    Interest: ($200); Silver Watches: ($20).

EARLY, JASON
    Land: 126 a. ($650); (Also paid for two free colored polls).

    EDMONDSON, WALTER (cont.)   voter

(Hotel)

    Interest: ($318); Silver Watches: ($30).

FLEETWOOD, DAVID est. (not given in)

FRAIM, JOHN G. (in the army)

GRIFFEN, JOHN B.

    Land: 2531 a. ($27000); Slaves: 68 ($24000); Interest: ($12190); Gold Watches: ($125); Piano: 1; Plate and Jewelry: ($80); Pleasure Vehicles: ($250); Household Furniture: ($650).

GRIMES, WM. T.   voter

    Interest: ($213); Silver Watches: ($20).

HARDY, H. H. est. (by W. T. Hancock)

    Land: 209 a. ($12100); Slaves: 7 ($20100).

HARDY, MARTHA T.

    Land: 250 a. ($5000); Slaves: 12 ($3600); Interest: ($448); Gold Watches: ($75); Piano: 1; Plate and Jewelry: ($25); Pleasure Vehicles: ($130); Household Furniture: ($250).

HARDY, THOMAS B.

    Land: 200 a. ($2500); Slaves: 17 ($5500); Gold Watches: ($75); Piano: 1; Plate and Jewelry: ($40); Pleasure Vehicles: ($200); Household Furniture: ($150).

HARDY, WM. A., DR.

HARRELL, JOHN   voter

    Interest: ($106).

HARRELL, JNO. B.   voter

    Interest: ($70).

(Hotel)

HILL, J. ANTHONY

    Land: Halifax County 1850 a. ($25000); Slaves: 61 ($18500).

HILL, WM. R. MISS

    Slaves: 42 ($14700); Interest: ($26500).

HOWARD, WILEY   voter

JENKINS, EMILY

    Land: 650 a. ($7500); Slaves: 13 ($4000); Piano: 1; Plate and Jewelry: ($16); Pleasure Vehicles: ($75); Household Furniture: ($300).

JENKINS, JOHN W. (by adv.)

    Interest: ($848).

JOHNSON, J. MILLAN

    Land: ½ a. ($500).

JOHNSON, J. P.   voter

    Interest: ($10600); Pleasure Vehicles: ($60).

JOLLIFF, L. C. MISS (by guardian)

    Slaves: 6 ($2800); Gold Watches: ($75).

JONES, THOMAS

    Land: 2341 a. ($27250) in Martin County.

LEE, I. B. est. (by Wm. S. Tayloe)

    Land: 9114 a. ($10000); Slaves: 33 ($13600).

LEE, JOS. W. (by Wm. S. Tayloe)

    Gold Watches: ($75).

(Hotel)

LEE, WM. C.

    Land: 844 a. ($7600); Slaves: 28 ($8400); Gold Watches: ($50);
    Piano: 1; Plate and Jewelry: ($25); Pleasure Vehicles: ($250);
    Household Furniture: ($250).

LINTON, RACHEL

    Land: 48 a. ($200).

MEAZZELL, AUGUSTUS   voter

    Land: 126 a. ($1000); Slave: 1 ($100); Interest: ($212).

MEAZZELL, JONATHAN   voter

MITCHELL, G. M.   voter

    Land: 15 a. ($1200); Interest: ($318); Gold Watches: ($15);
    Pleasure Vehicles: ($75).

PAGE, WM. H. est.

    Land: 150 a. ($750); Slaves: 3 ($600).

PARKER, JOHN A. (in the army)

PEELE, WM. H.   voter

    Land: 750 a. ($6000); Slaves: 11 ($5000); Pleasure Vehicles: ($75).

PITTMAN, E. D. (not given in)

POWELL, JAS. M.   voter

    Interest: ($2114); Gold Watches: ($60); Pleasure Vehicles: ($75).

POWELL, JESSIE A.

    Land: 609 a. ($8200); Slaves: 38 ($13450); Interest: ($8480);
    Household Furniture: ($200).

(Hotel)

POWELL, MARY J. KENNETH (not given in)

POWELL, RODDICK (not given in)

POWELL, WM. C.   voter

    Slaves: 3 ($650); Interest: ($2862); Gold Watches: ($110); Piano: 1; Pleasure Vehicles: ($60).

PRICE, WM. A.   voter

PUGH, JOS. J.   voter

    Land: 2200 a. ($22000); Slaves: 66 ($11500); Interest: ($2120); Gold Watches: ($150); Piano: 1; Plate and Jewelry: ($50); Pleasure Vehicles: ($150); Household Furniture: ($300).

PUGH, THO. J.

    Land: 1186 a. ($14400); Slaves: 47 ($12240); Gold Watches: ($70); Piano: 1; Plate and Jewelry: ($20); Pleasure Vehicles: ($125); Household Furniture: ($600).

PUGH, WHIT

PUGH, WHIT S.   voter

    Land: 890 a. ($10000); Slaves: 38 ($12500); Gold Watches: ($75); Plate and Jewelry: ($30); Pleasure Vehicles: ($75).

RAWLS, MOORE

    Land: 10 a. ($150).

RHEY, JOHN   voter

    Interest: ($318); (Also paid for one free colored poll).

ROGERS, JAS. E.   voter

    Slaves: 2 ($1000); Interest: ($53); Pleasure Vehicles: ($75).

(Hotel)

ROOKS, LAWRENCE

    Land: 20 a. ($100); (Also paid for one free colored poll).

RUFFIN, RACHEL

    Land: 2000 a. ($15000); Slaves: 66 ($12250); Plate and Jewelry: ($35); Pleasure Vehicles: ($100); Household Furniture: ($600).

RUFFIN, SARAH A. (not given in)

SAVAGE, WM. E. (by guardian)

    Land: 520 a. ($2500); Slaves: 16 ($4800); Interest: ($1900); Pleasure Vehicles: ($100).

SAVAGE, WM. R. (by M. E. G. Barrett)

    Land: 250 a. ($2500); Slaves: 13 ($3300).

SHERWOOD, JNO. J.

    Land: Martin County 656 a. ($6560).

SHOULARS, ELIZABETH

    Slaves: 4 ($1100).

SHOULARS, GEORGE J.   voter

    Land: 140 a. ($1000); Slaves: 13 ($4000); Silver Watches: ($35); Pleasure Vehicles: ($50).

SIMPSON, KITNCHEN (not given in)

SMALLWOOD, CHARLES, DR.   voter

    Land: 1100 a. ($9880); Slaves: 53 ($18800); Interest: ($2268); Gold Watches: ($75); Plate and Jewelry: ($40); Pleasure Vehicles: ($450); Household Furniture: ($175).

SMALLWOOD, JNO. R.

    Land: 1800 a. ($18000); Slaves: 56 ($18000); Interest: ($37000); Gold Watches: ($50).

(Hotel)

SMALLWOOD, ROBT. W.   voter

    Land: 260 a. ($2600); Slaves: 16 ($5000); Gold Watches: ($75); Pleasure Vehicles: ($25).

SMITH, ABRAM minor heirs (Not given in)

SMITH, JAS. A   voter

    Interest: ($212); Silver Watches: ($12).

SMITH, THO. J. est. (by Dr. Chas. Smallwood)

    Interest: ($1378).

SMITH, TREACEY

    Land: 618 a. ($5000); Slaves: 16 ($4800); Piano: 1.

STALLINGS, JAMES

STALLINGS, NOAH   voter

    Silver Watches: ($25).

SULIVAN, ELISHA est. (not given in)

THOMPSON, HEZAKIAH

    Land: 1367 a. ($14000); Slaves: 41 ($12000).

THOMPSON, JOHN

    Land: 949 a. ($10000); Slaves: 3 ($1200).

THOMPSON, LEWIS A.

    Land: 1449 a. ($15000); Slaves: 52 ($17500).

THOMPSON, LEWIS (cont.)

(Hotel)

    Land: 3848 a. ($40000); Slaves: 113 ($30000); Interest: ($19121); Bank Dividends: Bank of North Carolina ($2212); Gates across highway: 1; Gold Watches: ($140); Piano: 1; Plate and Jewelry: ($200); Pleasure Vehicles: ($150); Household Furniture: ($500).

THOMPSON, THO. W.   voter

    Land: 66 a. ($132).

URQUHART, A. B.

    Land: 4220 a. ($40000); Slaves: 67 ($16500).

URQUHART, JAMES

    Land: 400 a. ($7000).

URQUHART, WHIT AND JAS.

    Land: 949 a. ($16000); Slaves: 75 ($19800).

WALTON, WM.   voter

    Land: 800 a. ($6000); Slaves: 24 ($9200); Gold Watches: ($200); Pleasure Vehicles: ($150); Household Furniture: ($125).

WATSON, ELIZABETH

    Slaves: 14 ($5000); Interest: ($2200); Gold Watches: ($65).

WATSON, ELIZABETH, MRS. AND CHILDREN (by W. H. Lee)

    Slaves: 1 ($300); Interest: ($2000).

WATSON, R. C., DR.

    Slaves: 5 ($1500).

WATSON, R. C. est.

(Hotel)

WATSON, WINNIE H.

    Land: 265 a. ($2250); Slaves: 11 ($3250); Gold Watches: ($60); Plate and Jewelry: ($20); Pleasure Vehicles: ($110); Household Furniture: ($350).

WATSON, WINNIE P.

    Slaves: 19 ($7500); Interest: ($2200); Piano: 1.

WEATHERSBEE, R. E. H.

    Land: Martin County 1050 a. ($6250).

WHITE, JAS. W.   voter

    Interest: ($424); Silver Watches: ($20).

WHITEHEAD, MICAJHA   voter

    Interest: ($848); Gold Watches: ($50); Silver Watches: ($10).

WILLIAMS, HENRY

WILLIAMS, H. F., DR.   voter

    Land: 100 a. ($4000); Slaves: 2 ($800); Interest: ($742); Gold Watches: ($175); Piano: 1; Plate and Jewelry: ($50); Pleasure Vehicles: ($150); Household Furniture: ($400).

WILLIAMS, JOS. J.

    Land: 1425 a. ($15000); Slaves: 26 ($10500).

WILLIAMS, JNO. P.

    Land: 1330 a. ($15000); Slaves: 26 ($17500).

WILLIAMS, MARY J.

    Land: 700 a. ($8000); Slaves: 7 ($2600).

(Hotel)

WILLIAMS, MARY W.

   Land: 640 a. ($7500); Slaves: 33 ($10500).

WILLIAMS, THOMAS

   Land: 1000 a. ($15000); Slaves: 54 ($9800); Gates across highway: 1.

WILLIAMS, WM. K. A.

   Land: 1804 a. ($22150); Slaves: (not listed) ($27000).

WILLIFORD, GEORGE est. (by M. E. G. Barrett)

   Land: 173 a. ($732); Slaves: 10 ($3000); Interest: ($1293).

WILLIFORD, MARTHA A.

   Land: 173 a. ($732); Slaves: 2 ($900); Pleasure Vehicles: ($50).

WINBON, JNO. HENRY

WORLEY, WM. A.   voter

   Land: 224 a. ($1600); Slaves: 11 ($2725); Silver Watches: ($25).

(Hotel)

Total Taxable Property:

Land: 62,093½ a. - $565,376

Slaves: 1,624 - $519,895

Interest received or due: $144,524

Bank Dividends received or due: $2,212

Physicians: $2,000

Gates across highway: 2

Gold Watches: $2,085

Silver Watches: $352

Pianos: 13

Plate and Jewelry: $681

Pleasure Vehicles: $3,925

Household Furniture: $5,470

Total Value: $1,246,450

Total number of white voters: 43

Total number of colored voters: 5

Total people listed: 124

"The tax list taken by me in Hotel district is correct to the best of my knowledge and beleaf."

Wm. H. Lee

JERNIGAN DISTRICT

BRYAN, JOSEPH

BUTLER, JOHN

BUTLER, WM.
　　Land: 150 a. ($325).

BUTLER, WM. J.

CHERRY, GEORGE O. (by Joseph B. Cherry)
　　Land: 180 a. ($3000); Slaves: 18 ($4300); Pleasure Vehicles: ($50).

COWAN, JOHNSON

DUNDELOW, ?LMORE
　　Land: 120 a. ($250).

HARRISON, GEORGE

HARRISON, KADER

HOGGARD, DAVID　　　　　　　　　　　　　　　　　　　　　　voter
　　Land: 90 a. ($150).

HOGGARD, JOHN　　　　　　　　　　　　　　　　　　　　　　voter
　　Land: 175 a. ($300).

JERNIGAN, GEORGE
　　Land: 486 a. ($700).

(Jernigan)

JERNIGAN, NATHANIEL

    Land: 100 a. ($150); Slaves: 1 ($490).

    for Elizabeth White   Land: 100 a. ($300); Slaves: 13 ($3650); Interest: ($40).

JERNIGAN, ROLAND B.

    Land: 92 a. ($102).

JERNIGAN, SARIAH

    Land: 100 a. ($150); Slaves: 3 ($1200); Interest: ($400).

JERNIGAN, WM. J.   voter

    Land: 120 a. ($200).

JERNIGAN, WORLEY M.

LASITOR, JOHN

    Land: 569 a. ($900).

MILLER, JESTINA   voter

    Land: 222 a. ($200); Slaves: 1 (no value).

MIRES, GEORGE W.   voter

    Land: 188 a. ($500); Slaves: 1 ($150).

MITCHEAL, DARIUS   voter

    Land: 50 a. ($125); Silver Watches: ($5).

MITCHEAL, ELIZABETH

    Interest: ($310).

(Jernigan)

MITCHEAL, HENRY C.   voter
    Land: 100 a. ($250); Slaves: 1 ($450); Silver Watches: ($5).

MITCHEAL, MARY H.
    Slaves: 1 ($350); Interest: ($635).

MITCHEAL, REBECAH
    Land: 75 a. ($200); Interest: ($190).

MIZELL, MATTHEW T.
    Land: 133 a. ($200); Slaves: 5 ($1100).

MORRIS, ALFORD J.   (see Matthew H. Morris).

MORRIS, ELIJAH   voter
    Land: 75 a. ($100).

MORRIS, JAMES B.   (see Matthew H. Morris).

MORRIS, MATTHEW H.   voter
    Slaves: 4 ($1200); Silver Watches: ($10).
    for James B. Morris Estate   Slaves: 2 ($600).
    do Alford J. Morris   Land: 900 a. ($1400); Slaves: 11 ($2750); Pleasure Vehicles: ($50).

POWELL, LEVIN
    Land: 60 a. ($90).

(Jernigan)

TODD, ELISHA   voter
    Land: 100 a. ($150).

TODD, HAYWOOD   voter
    Land: 60 a. ($100).

TODD, JOHN D.   voter
    Land: 137 a. ($350).

TODD, LEVENIA   voter
    Land: 179 a. ($350); Slaves: 6 ($1700).

TODD, LEWIS   voter
    Land: 90 a. ($200).

TODD, MOSES   voter
    Land: 137 a. ($350).

WATSON, CELIA ESTATE   (by Joseph B. Cherry)
    Slaves: 6 ($1800).

WHITE, ABNER A.
    Land: 691 a. ($1100); Slaves: 1 ($450); Interest: ($1000).

WHITE, DUREN
    Land: 339 a. ($900); Slaves: 8 ($2150); Interest: ($1000);
    Pleasure Vehicles: ($50).

    for Martha J. White   Land: 60 a. ($60); Slaves: 2 ($700);
    Interest: ($71).

(Jernigan)

WHITE, ELIZABETH   (see Nathaniel Jernigan)

WHITE, HENRY W.
    Land: 60 a. ($200); Silver Watches: ($5).
    for Mareus A. White Estate   Land: 75 a. ($125).

WHITE, JOHNSON S.
    Land: 348 a. ($550); Slaves: 4 ($1200); Interest: ($120).

WHITE, JOSEPH A.

WHITE, JOSIAH

WHITE, KADER, SR.   voter
    Land: 378 a. ($730); Slaves: 2 ($800).

WHITE, KADER, JR.
    Land: 150 a. ($150).

WHITE, LORENZO

WHITE, MAREUS A.   (see Henry W. White).

WHITE, MARTHA J.   (see Duren White).

WHITE, SALLY and IRYE W. WHITE
    Land: 180 a. ($600).

WHITE, WM. H.   voter
    Land: 42 a. ($84).

(Jernigan)

Total taxable property:

Land: 7111 a. - $15,591

Slaves: 90 - $25,040

Interest received or due: $3,766

Silver Watches: $25

Pleasure Vehicles: $150

Total Value: $44,572

Total number of voters: 17

Total people listed: 52

DURGAN DISTRICT

ASBEL, ALONZA   voter

    Land: 100 a. ($125).

BARNECASCEL, CHARLES   voter

BARNECASCEL, G. W.   voter

    Land: 75 a. ($262); Interest: $390.

BARNECASCEL, SAMUEL

    Land: 110 a. ($220); Interest: ($173).

BARNECASCEL, WM. S.   voter

    Land: 50 a. ($75); Interest: ($35).

BIRCH, JOSIPH J.   voter

BIRD, HENRY

    Land: 20 a. ($120).

BIRD, JAMES   voter

    Land: 20 a. ($120).

BIRD, WILLIAM   voter

    Land: 8 a. ($32).

BOND, DANIEL

    Interest: ($2674).

BOND, HENRY

    Interest: ($5213).

(Durgan)

BOND, HENRY and DANIEL
    Slaves: 11 ($5200).

BOWEN, WM. E.   voter

BRONSON, BENJAMIN
    Land: 250 a. ($1000); Slaves: 6 ($2700).

BUTLER, JOHN   voter
    Land: 50 a. ($75).

BUTLER, WILIMESON   voter
    Land: 50 a. ($300); 64 a. ($100).

BYRUM, STARKLY E.   free colored voter
    Land: 209 a. ($1056); Slaves: 1 ($450).

BYRUM, WILLIAM
    Land: 153 a. ($229).

CALE, DUNCAN L.
    Land: 572 a. ($784); Slaves: 1 ($400).

CANADA, BALADA   voter
    Land: 51 a. ($76).

CAPHART, CHARLES
    Land: 340 a. ($675); Interest: ($1400).

CAPHART, ROBBERT   voter

CAPS, JOHN   voter

2

(Durgan)

CASTLOW, ADDIN H.
    Land: 300 a. ($450); Slaves: 1 ($150).

CASTLOW, DORSEY   voter
    Land: 150 a. ($225).

CASTLOW, JAMES E.
    Land: 255 a. ($300).

CASTLOW, LARRY
    Land: 31 a. ($124).

CASTLOW, LARRY
    Land: 24 a. ($315).

CASTLOW, STARKEY   voter

CASTLOW, WILLIAM   voter
    Land: 75 a. ($112).

CASTLOW, WILLIAM
    Land: 60 a. ($60).

COBB, HENRY T.   voter

COBB, LOUIS
    Land: 90 a. ($135).

COBB, SAMUEL   voter
    Land: 345 a. ($690).

(Durgan)

CONNER, HORRET

    Land: 50 a. ($100).

CONNER, RICHARD J.

    Land: 224 a. ($480).

COOPPER, ANKINS

    Land: 30 a. ($60).

COOPPER, JOHN

    Land: 1948 a. ($7000); Slaves: 34 ($14600).

COOPPER, JOHNOTHAN heirs

    Land: 240 a. ($372).

COOPPER, JOHN and JOSEPH

    Land: 100 a. ($750).

COOPPER, JOSEPH

    Land: 2292 a. ($10000); Slaves: 92 ($31600); Interest: ($2000); Silver Watches: ($20); Plate and Jewelry: ($25); Pleasure Vehicles: ($150).

CULIPHER, ELIZABETH

    Land: 105 a. ($210); Interest: ($195).

CULIPHER, JACKSON   voter

CULIPHER, JAMES   voter

    Land: 210 a. ($300); Interest: ($441).

(Durgan)

CULIPHER, JAMES heirs

    Interest: ($966).

FERGUSON, LEE

    Interest: ($2000).

FERGUSON, WILLIAM A.   voter

    Land: 577 a. ($3853), Town Property ($1500); Slaves: 6 ($2325); Interest: ($150); Gold Watches: ($30); Piano: 1; Plate and Jewelry: ($30); Pleasure Vehicles: ($300).

FERGUSON, WILLIAM F.

    Land: 107 a. ($107); Slaves: 13 ($4660); Interest: ($1381).

GRAY, PENELIPIA estate

    Slaves: 13 ($5600).

GRAY, WILLIAM

    Land: 663 a. ($2500); Gold Watches: ($50).

GREGORY, THOMAS

    Land: 507 a. ($550).

HANESON, DOW   voter

    Land: 130 a. ($195).

HARREL, DAVID

    Land: 252 a. ($504); Silver Watches: ($20).

HECKSTALL, ELIZABETH

    Land: 350 a. ($1050); Slaves: 24 ($7300).

(Durgan)

HECKSTALL, JOHN W.   voter

   Land: 185 a. ($350); Slaves: 8 ($2800); Gold Watches: ($50).

HECKSTALL, THOMAS J.

   Land: 325 a. ($1138).

HECKSTALL, WILLIAM

   Land: 5 a. ($100).

HOGARD, CALVIN   voter

   Land: 79 a. ($158).

HOGARD, FROSUNE   voter

   Land: 200 a. ($480); Slaves: 1 ($200).

HOGARD, JOHN

   Land: 642 a. ($1700); Slaves: 13 ($4800).

HUGHS, JACOP E.   voter

   Land: 143 a. ($321); Interest: ($335).

JERNIGAN, AUGUSTUS

   Land: 50 a. ($87).

JERNIGAN, ENOCH   voter

   Land: 100 a. ($150).

JOHNSTON, HAWOOD   voter

   Land: 10 a. ($75).

6

(Durgan)

JOHNSTON, JOHN B.   voter
    Land: 65 a. ($97).

KEETAR, HUMPHREY   voter
    Land: 50 a. ($100).

LANGDALE, JAMES   voter
    Land: 276 a. ($828); Slaves: 6 ($1775).

LANGDALE, ROBBERT
    Land: 137 a. ($174).

LECESTER, MARY estate
    Land: 55 a. ($100); Interest: ($194).

MACK, DANIEL WM.   free colored voter
    Land: 50 a. ($100).

MADRA, JAMES heirs
    Interest: ($700).

McGLOHON, L. W.
    Land: 580 a. ($1040); Slaves: 6 ($2450); Pleasure Vehicles: ($50).

MIZELLS, ARON S.
    Land: 401 a. ($802); Slaves: 3 ($1200).

MIZELLS, DELLEA A.
    Land: 143 a. ($321); Interest: ($647).

(Durgan)

MIZELLS, ELI. T.   voter
    Land: 103 a. ($225); Interest: ($70).

MIZELLS, GEORGE   voter
    Land: 172 a. ($283).

MIZELLS, HANKS E.
    Land: 143 a. ($286); Interest: ($647).

MIZELLS, HENRY C.   voter
    Land: 525 a. ($1048); Interest: ($34); Silver Watches: ($15).

MIZELLS, HENRY T.   voter
    Land: 135 a. ($270).

MIZELLS, JOHN G.
    Land: 200 a. ($280) Slaves: 1 ($550); Interest: ($680).

MIZELLS, JOHN T.   voter
    Land: 143 a. ($321); Silver Watches: ($25).

MIZELLS, JOHNENTHON T.
    Land: 150 a. ($350).

MIZELLS, MILES   voter
    Land: 169 a. ($379); Interest: ($500).

MIZELLS, SOLOMON, JR.   voter
    Land: 275 a. ($500); Slaves: 2 ($800).

(Durgan)

MIZELLS, SOLOMAN, SR.   voter

    Land: 250 a. ($550).

MIZELLS, STARKY E.

    Land: 529 a. ($1300); Slaves: 4 ($1400); Interest: ($1875); Silver Watches: ($10); Pleasure Vehicles:($50).

MIZELLS, THOMAS T.   voter

    Land: 45 a. ($100).

MIZELLS, WM. W.   voter

    Land: 302 a. ($604); Slaves: 1 ($600).

MOORE, C. S.

    Land: 110 a. ($275); Pleasure Vehicles: ($100).

MOORE, J. C.

    Land: 380 a. ($776).

OVERTON, BITHA

    Land: 10 a. ($50).

PEELIE, WILLIAM A. estate

    Interest: ($400).

PEMPSY, JOSEPH   free colored voter

PHELPS, JOHN A.

    Land: 150 a. ($450); Slaves: 2 ($800); Interest: ($939).

(Durgan)

PHELPS, JOHN　　　　　　　　　　　　　　　　　　　　　voter
　　　Land: 125 a. ($220).

PIENENCE, DANIEL　　　　　　　　　　　　　　　　　　　voter
　　　Land: 64 a. ($96).

PIERCE, JAMES H.
　　　Land: 109 a. ($168).

PILAND,(?)　　　　　　　　　　　　　　　　　　　　　　voter
　　　Land: 500 a. ($500).

ROBERTSON, JOHN　　　　　　　　　　　　　　　　　　　voter
　　　Land: 114 a. ($239).

SIMONS, A. J.　　　　　　　　　　　　　　　　　　　　voter
　　　Land: 50 a. ($100).

SIMMONS, B. H.
　　　Land: 15 a. ($60).

SIMONS, DAVID L.　　　　　　　　　　　　　　　　　　　voter
　　　Land: 45 a. ($45).

SIMONS, HENRY　　　　　　　　　　　　　　　　　　　　voter

SIMMONS, Z. T.
　　　Land: 800 a. ($1500); Slaves: 20 ($7400).

SMITHWICK, THOMAS
　　　Land: 107 a. ($475); Silver Watches: ($7).

(Durgan)

TADLOCK, WILLIAM
    Land: 625 a. ($2000); Slaves: 8 ($3100).

THOMPSON, A. H.   voter
    Land: 80 a. ($120).

THOMPSON, B. W.
    Land: 65 a. ($130).

THOMPSON, MARCUS H.   voter

TOD, SAMUEL J.   voter
    Land: 86 a. ($86).

TODD, LEWIS   voter

TODD, SOLOMAN
    Land: 566 a. ($500).

WHITE, RIGHT H.   voter
    Land: 317 a. ($700); Interest: ($280).

WHITE, WILLIAM T.   voter
    Land: 50 a. ($87).

WILFORD, HARRY
    Land: 317 a. ($814); Interest: ($600).

WILFORD, JOHN   voter

(Durgan)

WILLIAMS, JOHN   voter

    Land: 100 a. ($300).

WINBON, J. W.   voter

    Land: 275 a. ($1500).

Total Taxable Property:

Land: 23,014 a. - $61,279

Slaves: 277 - $102,860

Interest Received or Due: $24,919

Silver Watches: $97

Gold Watches: $130

Piano: 1

Plate and Jewelry: $55

Pleasure Vehicles: $650

Total Value: $189,990

Total number of white voters: 55

Total number of colored voters: 3

Total people listed: 118

DURGAN DISTRICT MILITARY ROLL

Asbel, Alonza
Barnesascel, W^m. S.
Birch, Josiph J.
Bird, James
Bird, William
Bowen, W^m. E.
Butler, John
Butler, Williamson
Cale, Duncan L.
Canada, Balada
Caphart, Robbert
Caps, John
Castlow, Dorsey
Castlow, Starky
Castlow, Williams
Cobb, Henry T.
Cobb, Samuel
Culipher, Jackson
Culipher, James
Ferguson, William A.
Gray, William
Haneson, Dow
Hogard, Calvin
Hogard, Frosune
Hughs, Jacop E.
Jernigan, Augustus
Johnston, Enoch

Johnston, Hawood
Keeta, Humphrey
Langdale, John
MiZells, Eli T.
MiZells, Henry C.
MiZells, Henry T.
MiZells, John T.
MiZells, Miles
MiZells, Thomas T.
MiZells, W^m. W.
MiZells, George
Pierce, Daniel
Piland, Arodi
Robertson, John
Simons, A. J.
Simons, David L.
Simons, Henry
Smithwick, Thomas
Thompson, A. H.
Tod, Samuel J.
Todd, Lewis
White, William T.
White, Write H.
Wilford, John
Williams, John
Winbon, J. W.

COLERAIN DISTRICT

ASKEW, CAROLINE (see Taylor, Hillory).

ASKEW, DAVID C.   voter

    Land: 274 a. ($1644); Slaves: 2 ($600); Silver Watches: ($15);
    Pleasure Vehicles: ($60).

ASKEW, DAVID C. (adv., R. Jones)

    Land: 100 a. ($500); Slaves: 13 ($2600).

ASKEW, GEO. W. (see Taylor, Hillory).

ASKEW, J. A. J.   voter

    Land: Town Lots 2 ($3000); Slaves: 10 ($2500); Interest: ($400);
    Silver Watches: ($20); Pleasure Vehicles: ($50).
    do for Jacob Perry heirs   Interest: ($504).

ASKEW, JR. E. (see Etheridge, Jos. H.).

ASKEW, J. W. (see Etheridge, Jos. H.).

ASKEW, JOS. W.

ASKEW, JOSEPH H.   (see Etheridge, Jos. H.).

ASKEW, LAWRENCE (adv., A. J. Jones)

    Land: 100 a. ($500); Slaves: 3 ($750).

ASKEW, LEVI (Guardian A. Gaskins heirs)

    Land: 100 a. ($500).

ASKEW, MARTHA E. (see Etheridge, Jos. H.).

ASKEW, WM. D. (see Etheridge, Jos. H.).

(Colerain)

ASKEW, PRISCILLA (not listed).

BAKER, JOHN (not listed).

BAKER, LEMUEL (not listed).

BALANCE, JANE (not listed).

BEASLEY, JOS. W.   voter

    Land: 200 a. ($1075); Slaves: 12 ($3000); Silver Watches: ($10).
    do for Jos. Thomps. heirs   Land: 125 a. ($500); Interest: ($1700).
    do for Morris. heirs   Land: 200 a. ($1000); Slaves: 13 ($2600);
    Interest: ($440).

BEASLEY, THOS. SR.

    Land: 50 a. ($300); Slaves: 6 ($1200); Interest: ($661).

BEASLEY, THOS. JR.   voter

    Land: 182 a. ($942); Slaves: 7 ($1750); Interest: ($260); Silver
    Watches: ($5).

BELCH, WILLIAM   voter

    Land: 125 a. ($750).

BIRD, WILLIN

    Land: $31\frac{1}{4}$ a. ($250).

BROWN, THOS. W.   voter

    Land: 108 a. ($864); Silver Watches: ($12).

BUNCH, JNO. A.

CHERRY, MARY A. MRS. (cont.)

(Colerain)

 Land: 50 a. ($300); Slaves: 14 ($3500); Bank Dividends: ($240);
 Bank: Windsor Bank; Gold Watches: ($100); Pleasure Vehicles: ($100).

EDGE, SALLY (not listed).

ELLYSON, ZECHERIAH

ETHERIDGE, JOS. H. (home)   voter

 Land: home 1800 a. ($25000), Cherry farm in Windsor- no value, Perry
 and White town 500 a. ($1000); Slaves: 240 ($60000); Interest: ($1000);
 Bank Dividends: ($475); Bank: Windsor Bank; Stud Horses and Jacks:
 1; Gold Watches: ($100); Silver Watches: ($10); Pianos: 1; Pleasure Vehicles: ($100); Household and Kitchen Furniture: ($800).

 guardian for E. Askew Jr. Interest: ($2061).

 do for J. W. Askew Interest: ($1411).
 do for Martha E. Askew Interest: ($1786).
 do for Joseph H. Askew Interest: ($1550).
 do for Wm. D. Askew Interest: ($1708).

ETHERIDGE, WM. D.

 Land: 1665 a. ($10860); Slaves: 41 ($10250); Pleasure Vehicles:
 ($50).

EVANS, LEMUEL

 Land: Hertford (County) 239 a. ($1165).

FELLOWS, ODD

 Land: Town Lots 1 ($800).

FREEMAN, JAMES   voter

 Land: 78 a. ($468); Slaves: 2 ($500).

FREEMAN, JNO. B.   voter

 Land: 223 a. ($1115); Slaves: 2 ($900).

(Colerain)

GARRETT, JAMES F.   voter

    Land: 271 a. ($1626); Slaves: 3 ($1200).

GASKINS, A. heirs (see Askew, Levi).

GODWIN, JAMES C.   voter

    Land: 310 a. ($1860); Slaves: 2 ($700); Silver Watches: ($12);
    Pleasure Vehicles: ($50).

HARRELL, BEDDICK, SR.

    Land: 150 a. ($1050); Slaves: 7 ($2000).

HARRELL, BEDDICK, JR. (not listed).

HARRELL, DOSSEY   voter

    Land: 50 a. ($250).

HARRELL, ISSAC   voter

    Land: 25 a. ($100).

HARRELL, JAMES

    Land: 78 a. ($390).

HARRELL, JOHN (not listed).

HARRELL, NOAH

    Land: 20 a. ($100).

HAYS, WILIN D.

    Land: 200 a. ($1000); Town Lots (2) ($3500); Slaves: 9 ($2250);
    Interest: ($610); Gold Watches: ($85); Pleasure Vehicles: ($125);
    Household and Kitchen Furniture: ($260).

(Colerain)

HENRY, B. R. heirs (see Henry, Peyton T. Jr.).

HENRY, PEYTON T. JR.   voter

    Land: 96 a. ($1010), Town Lots (1) ($2500); Slaves: 1 ($250).
    do for heirs B. R. Henry   Land: 300 a. ($1800); Slaves: 6 ($1500).

HOLLOWMAN, JESTON

    Land: 50 a. ($100).

JONES, CELVIN, MRS.

    Land: 234 a. ($1404); Slaves: 4 ($800); Pleasure Vehicles: ($100).

JONES, LEVENIA, MRS.

    Land: 100 a. ($600).

LANE, GEORGE W.

    Land: 930 a. ($5580); Slaves: 27 ($6750).

LANE, HARRY W.   voter

    Land: 234 a. ($1404); Pleasure Vehicles: ($50); Household and Kitchen Furniture: ($300).

MILLER, ELIZABETH, MRS.

    Land: 8 a. ($40).

MILLER, JOSIAH

    Land: 21 a. ($105).

MILLER, SOLLOWINAU

    Land: 200 a. ($800); Slaves: 8 ($1750); Interest: ($190).

MIZELL, JOSIAH (cont.)   voter

(Colerain)

    Land: 523 a. ($2915); Town Lots (2) ($4500); Slaves: 47 ($10515); Interest: ($5885); Gold Watches: ($120); Pianos: 1; Pleasure Vehicles: ($275); Household Furniture: ($400).

MORRIS heirs (see Beasley, Jos. W.).

MORRIS, CALVIN, J.   voter

    Pleasure Vehicles: ($75).

MORRIS, ELI (not listed).

MORRIS, JAMES L.

    Land: 109 a. ($654); Slaves: 11 ($1700).

NORTHCOTT, ANDREW

    Land: 707 a. ($3556); Slaves: 14 ($3500); Interest: ($934); Bank Dividends: ($400); Bank: Windsor Bank; Pleasure Vehicles: ($100); Household Furniture: ($300).

NORTHCOTT, JOS. H.   voter

    Silver Watches: ($10); Pleasure Vehicles: ($75).

NORTHCOTT, WM. T.   voter

    Interest: ($315); Silver Watches: ($10).

NOWELL, SETH FOR JOS. (not listed).

OUTLAW, BRITTON (not listed).

OUTLAW, HEZEKIAH (not listed).

OUTLAW, JEREMIAH

    Land: 125 a. ($1625); Slaves: 10 ($250); Interest: ($500); Gold Watches: ($50); Pleasure Vehicles: ($100).

(Colerain)

OUTLAW, WM. D.   voter

OUTLAW, WM. J.   voter
    Land: 150 a. ($750).

OUTLAW, WILSON
    Land: 133 a. ($798); Slaves: 12 ($3060).

PEAL, ALEXANDER   voter
    Interest: ($50).

PEAL, AMOS
    Land: 65 a. ($520); Interest: ($360).

PEAL, EDITH J.
    Land: 64 a. ($640); Interest: ($110).

PEAL, JOSEPH L.   voter
    Land: 50 a. ($300); Silver Watches: ($15).

PEARCE, HENRY
    Land: 100 a. ($500).

PERRY, ETHERTON   voter
    Land: 365 a. ($2166); Slaves: 15 ($3750); Gold Watches: ($100).

PERRY, GEORGE W.
    Land: 195 a. ($1265); Slaves: 11 ($2425); Interest: ($740); Gold Watches: ($50).

PERRY, ISSAC
    Land: 709 a. ($4204); Slaves: 10 ($2500); Interest: ($417).
    do for Wrights heirs   Interest: ($2158).

7

(Colerain)

PERRY, JACOB heirs (see Askew, J. A. J.).

PERRY, JANE
 Land: 50 a. ($100).

PERRY, JOSEPH J. (not listed)
 do-

PERRY, MARTHA A. (see Perry, Zecheriah).

PERRY, MARTHA A. SNIPS
 Land: 50 a. ($100); Slaves: 2 ($600); Interest: ($1160).

PERRY, MARY E.
 Land: 50 a. ($100); Slaves: 2 ($500); Interest: ($700).

PERRY, SHADY   voter
 Land: 239 a. ($3107); Slaves: 7 ($1500); Silver Watches: ($25); Pleasure Vehicles: ($50).

PERRY, SHADY
 Land: 380 a. ($380).

PERRY, TURNER   voter
 Land: 110 a. ($550).

PERRY, WM. D.

PERRY, WM D.   voter
 Land: 232 a. ($3016); Slaves: 3 ($750); Interest: ($623); Silver Watches: ($8).

(Colerain)

PERRY, ZECHERIAH   voter

    Land: 163 a. ($652).
    do for Guardian Martha A. Perry   Interest: ($70).

PERVIS, HENRY (not listed).

POWELL, HEZCEKIAH   voter

    Land: 125 a. ($500), Town Lots (1) ($3000); Slaves: 8; Interest:
    ($1600); Gold Watches: ($80); Pleasure Vehicles: ($90); Household
    Furniture: ($460).

PRUDEN, KINCHEN T.

    Land: 162 a. ($878); Slaves: 5 ($1300); Interest: ($1355); Silver
    Watches: ($15); Pleasure Vehciles: ($50).

SESSOMS, JNO. W.   voter

    Interest: ($782); Gold Watches: ($50).

SIMONS, E. P.   voter

    Land: 774 a. ($5250); Slaves: 28 ($6440); Interest: ($2787); Gold
    Watches: ($25); Silver Watches: ($25); Pianos: 1; Pleasure Vehicles:
    ($200); Household Furniture: ($200).

SNIPS, ELENOR HARDY

    Slaves: 42 ($10500); Interest: ($12000); Gold Watches: ($125);
    Pianos: 1.

SNIPS, MARY E. BROWN

    Slaves: 1 ($150); Pianos: 1.

SPRUILL, SAMUL B.

    Land: 1972 a. ($19720); Slaves: 67 ($16750); Gold Watches: ($150);
    Pleasure Vehicles: ($300); Household Furniture: ($1500).

(Colerain)

TAYLOR, HILLORY GUARDIAN   (not listed)

    do for Geo. W. Askew
    do for Caroline Askew

THOMPSON, EMMA E.

    Interest: ($500).

THOMPS. JOS. heirs   (see Beasley, Jos. W.).

VALENTINE, DAVID A.   voter

    Land: 229 a. ($1372); Slaves: 8 ($975); Interest: ($497).

WATFORD, JOSEPH J.   voter

    Land: 410 a. ($1542); Slaves: 11 ($2750); Interest: ($200); Gold Watches: ($100); Pleasure Vehciles: ($75).

WHITE, BACHEL   (see Wilson, Etherton).

WHITE, MR. E   (see Wilson, John).

WHITE, ISSAC

    Land: 468 a. ($4680); Slaves: 21 ($5250); Silver Watches: ($2); Household Furniture: ($225).

WHITE, JOSEPH   (see Wilson, Etherton).

WHITE, JOSIAH SR.

    Land: 1933 a. ($15070); Slaves: 30 ($7500); Interest: ($1515); Pianos: 1; Pleasure Vehicles: ($300); Household Furniture: ($375).

WHITE, JOSIAH JR.

    Land: 231 a. ($1617); Slaves: 2 ($500); Interest: ($500); Pleasure Vehicles: ($100).

(Colerain)

WHITE, JOS. B. (not listed).

WHITE, MARTHA W. (see Wilson, John).

WILLIAMS, JOHN for wife

    Land: 100 a. ($500); Slaves: 4 ($800); Interest: ($675).

WILSON, ETHERTON

    Land: 900 a. ($9000); Slaves: 28 ($7000); Interest: ($4603); Bank Dividends: ($24); Bank: Branch Bank of Windsor, N. C.; Gold Watches: ($50); Pianos: 1; Pleasure Vehicles: ($200); Household Furniture: ($500).
    do for Joseph White   Interest: ($534).
    do for Rachel White   Interest: ($503).

WILSON, JOHN   voter

    Land: 979 a. ($9790); Slaves: 32 ($8000); Interest: ($2000); Gold Watches: ($50); Silver Watches: ($20); Pianos: 1; Pleasure Vehicles: ($200); Household Furniture: ($375).
    do for Guardian Mr. E. White   Land: 2536 a. ($6000); Slaves: 74 ($18500); Interest: ($13621).
    do for Martha W. White   Interest: ($14865).

WILSON, SILAS

    Land: 243 a. ($2976); Slaves: 11 ($2200); Interest: ($1200).

WINBORNE, WATSON S.

    Land: 215 a. ($675).

WRIGHTS HEIRS (see Perry, Issac).

(Colerain)

Total Taxable Property:

Land: 25,273¼ a. - $175,420

Town Lots: 9 - $17,300

Slaves: 948 - $227,075

Interest received or due: $88,040

Bank Dividends received or due: $779

Stud Horses: 6

Gold Watches: $1,235

Silver Watches: $214

Pianos: 8

Pleasure Vehciles: $2,875

Household Furniture: $5,695

Total Value: $518,633

Total number of white voters: 34

Total number of people listed: 116

WHITE'S DISTRICT

ASKEW, CULLIN

    Land: 95a. ($200).

BAKER, HENRY   voter

    Land: 407a. ($457).

    do for George and Gilbert Baker   Land: 204a. ($204).

BAKER, GEORGE and GILBERT (see Henry Baker).

BIRDE, JOSIAH

    Land: 220a. ($220).

BIRDE, ROBERT W.

    Land: 75a. ($75).

BIRDE, WM. W.   voter

    Land: 75a. ($112).

BOWEN, JAMES H. (in the army).

BROWN, JACKSON   voter

    Land: 400a. ($600).

BROWN, WILLIAM   voter

    Land: 300a. ($450).

BRYANT, DAVID

    Land: 155a. ($124).

(White's)

BULTER, KADES   voter
    Land: 73a. ($153).

CASTELLOW, Q. T. (not 21).
    Land: 300a. ($600).

CASTELLOW, STARKEY
    Land: 161a. ($200).

COBB, CHANY
    Land: 111a. ($487).

COBB, GEORGE W.   voter
    Land: 200a. ($200).

COBB, JAMES H.   voter

COBB, JONATH.
    Land: 35a. ($35).

COBB, WILLIAM   voter
    Land: 111a. ($140).

COFFIELD, HENRY E. (in the army)
    Land: 125a. (no value listed); Slaves: 3 ($900).

COFFIELD, LUKE
    Land: 187a. ($450); Slaves: 2 ($600); Interest: ($15).

COFFIELD, THOMAS B. (in the army).

(White's)

CORBITT, JAMES H.   voter
    Land: 100a. ($150).

CORBITT, WILLIAM
    Land: 370a. ($500); Interest: ($700).

CRUMMY, KADES (in the army)
    Land: 200a. ($200).

CULLIFER, FRUZY
    Land: 58a. ($100).

EVANS, JAMES
    Land: 260a. ($450).

EVANS, JONATHAN   voter
    Land: 300a. ($450).

EVANS, STARKEY   voter
    Land: 581a. ($875).

FARLESS, HENRY   voter
    Land: 315a. ($660); Interest: ($433).

FLOYD, WINBORN
    Land: 50a. ($75).

FRANCIS, CHARLES E.   voter

FRANCIS, JAMES H.   voter
    Land: 128a. ($281); Slaves: 2 ($900).

(White's)

FRANCIS, MOSSES, DR.   voter

FRANCIS, WILLIAM F. (too olde).

GASKINS, DAVID

    Land: 837a. ($4000); Slaves: 34 ($10200); Interest: ($1950);
Piano: 1; Pleasure Vehicles: ($325); Household Furniture: ($107).

GASKINS, GEORGE L.   voter

GASKINS, JOHN S.   voter

    Silver Watch: ($20).

GASKINS, MARY

    Land: 277a. ($1500); Slaves: 14 ($5600); Interest: ($480);
Pleasure Vehicles: ($75); Household Furniture: ($100).

GASKINS, WM. T.   voter

GREGORY, ALFRED J.   voter

    Interest: ($70).

GREGORY, DAVID

    Land: 120a. ($300).

GREGORY, JOHN T. (in the army).

GREGORY, WILLIAM L. (in the army)

    Land: 3a. ($30).

HALSEY, CULLIN A.

    Land: 210a. ($675); Interest: ($111).

(White's)

HARE, CATHARINE
    Land: 25a. ($70).

HARRELL, DAVID J. (in the army).

HARRELL, ISAAC W.   voter

HENRY, ANS. D.
    Interest: ($50).

HENRY, CELIA
    Land: 45a. ($135); Interest: ($325).

HENRY, JOHN   voter
    Land: 356a. ($820); Slaves: 1 ($600); Interest: ($525).
    for M. H. Henry Land: 130a. ($325).

HENRY, M. H. (see John Henry).

HENRY, ROBT. M.
    Land: 59a. ($60); Interest: ($50).

HOGGARD, ELISHA   voter
    Land: 200a. ($200).

HOGGARD, DAVID
    Land: 742a. ($1025).

HOGGARD, HENRY   voter

HOGGARD, GEORGE G.   voter

(White's)

HOGGARD, TIMOTHY   voter

    Land: 50a. ($100).

HOLLEY, AUGUSTUS

    Land: 7579a. ($46300); Slaves: 160 ($48000); Interest: ($1600); Dentist: ($6); Gold Watch: ($50); Piano: 1; Plates & Jewelry: ($25); Pleasure Vehicles: ($800); Household Furniture: ($600).

HOLLEY and PILAND

    Interest: ($2500).

HOLLEY, THOS., DR.   voter

    Land: 400a. ($300); Silver Watch: ($25).

HOLLEY, THOS. J.   voter

    Land: 1500a. ($12000); Slaves: 43 ($12900); Gold Watch: ($100); Household Furniture: ($100).

HUGHES, DAVID D. (in the army).

HUGHES, GEORGE R.

HUGHES, GRANDISON (dead in the army).

HUGHES, JOHN (in the army).

HUGHES, MILES

HUGHES, MILES H.   voter

    Land: 200a. ($150); Interest: ($25).

HUGHES, RIDDICK (in the army).

(White's)

HUGHES, SARAH
    Land: 100a. ($150).

HUGHES, WHITMILL H.   voter
    Land: 100a. ($300).

JERONAGIN, HENRY P.   voter
    Land: 100a. ($150).

LAWRENCE, A., HEIRS (see Jas. Leary).

LEARY, JAS. for JAS. and FRANK RAYNER
    Slaves: 5 ($1500); Interest: ($3435).
    do for Lawrence, A., Heirs   Slaves: 7 ($2100); Interest ($1900).

LEARY, JAMES E. (in the army).

LEARY, JOHN W.   voter

LEARY, JOSEPH
    Land: 977a. ($4225); Slaves: 27 ($8000).

MCGLAUHON, JOHN R.   voter
    Silver Watch: ($20).

MCGLAUHON, WM. F.
    Land: 470a. ($1880); Slaves: 2 ($900); Household Furniture: ($50).
    do Guardians for Miss A. E. ? Slaves: (not listed) ($266).

MILLER, AQUELLA
    Slaves: 9 ($2700).

(White's)

MILLER, ISAAC W. (in the army)
    Land: 100a. ($150).

MILLER, JAS. A.
    Land: 100a. ($100).

MILLER, J. B.   voter
    Land: 50a. ($100).

MILLER, JOHN H. (in the army).

MILLER, PENELOPE
    Land: 96a. ($240); Slaves: 5 ($1500); Interest: ($27).

MILLER, WRC   voter
    Interest: ($50); Silver Watch: ($5).

MILLER, WORLEY
    Land: 200a. ($250); Slaves: 6 ($1800).

MIZELL, AARON
    Land: 96a. ($200).

MIZELL, AARON T.   voter
    Land: 60a. ($79); Interest: ($25); Silver Watch: ($10).

MIZELL, ELIZABETH
    Land: 82a. ($123).

MIZELL, GEORGE (in the army).

(White's)

MIZELL, JONATHAN

    Land: 530a. ($1530); Slaves: 1 ($600).

MIZELL, JOHN D.   voter

    Land: 120a. ($200); Silver Watch: ($10).

MIZELL, JUDAH

    Land: 60a. ($79).

MIZELL, WILLIAM (in the amry and no land).

MORGAN, ELIZABETH

MORRIS, JOSEPH H.

    Land: 226a. ($585); Slaves: 4 ($1200); Interest: ($622); Silver Watch: ($8).

MORRIS, WILLIAM S.   voter

    Slaves: 1 ($600); Interest: ($134); Silver Watch: ($8).

NEWBERN, ETHERTON

    Land: 38a. ($125); Interest: ($200).

NEWBERN, HENDERSON (in the army).

NEWBERN, HUNTER

NEWBERN, JOHN, SNR.

    Land: 50a. ($150).

NEWBERN, JOHN, JR.

    Land: 125a. ($275).

(White's)

NEWBERN, THOMAS (in the army).

NIXON, AUGUSTUS   voter

NIXON, JAMES A. (in the army).

NIXON, JOHN (in the army).

NOWEL, JOSIAH (in the army).

ONLY, WM. D. (in the army).

PEARCE, ISAAC   voter
    Land: 264a. ($460).

PEARCE, JAS. H. and DAVID N.
    Land: 357a. ($357).

PELAND, ISAAC
    Land: 50a. ($50); Slaves: not listed ($200); Gold Watch: ($30);
    Pleasure Vehicles: ($75).

PERRY, ABNER

PERRY, CHRISTAIN
    Land: 140a. ($700); Slaves: 5 ($1500).

PERRY, FOREMAN   voter

PERRY, JACOB B.   voter
    Land: 50a. ($200); Interest: ($400).

(White's)

PERRY, JOHN

    Land: 175a. ($940); Slaves: 1 ($400).

PERRY, JOHN A.   voter

PERRY, JOHN L.   voter

    Land: 70a. ($105); Slaves: 1 ("worthless").

PERRY, JOSEPH H.   voter

    Land: 50a. ($100).

PERRY, JOSIAH (in the amry).

PERRY, MARCUS W.   voter

    Land: 53a. ($212); Slaves: 1 ($300).

PERRY, MARTIN   voter

    Land: 50a. ($75).

PERRY, THOMAS (in the army)

    Land: 100a. ($100).

PERRY, WILLIAM D. (in the amry)

    Land: 102a..($102).

RAYNER, JAS. and FRANK (see James E. Leary).

SMITH, LEWIS

    Land: 225a. ($900); Slaves: 5 ($1500); Interest: ($100).

SMITH, JAMES

(White's)

SMITH, MARTHA

for SOUTH'S HEIRS (see George W. Ward).

THOMAS, LEWIS   voter
    Land: 140a. ($140).

THOMAS, JOSEPH

TODD, JAMES
    Land: 56a. ($168).

TODD, MOSSES
    Land: 25a. ($50).

TODD, SARAH
    Land: 9a. ($9).

WARD, GEORGE W.
    Land: 171a. ($350); Slaves: 3 ($900); Interest: ($350).

    do for South's Heirs Slaves: 4 ($1200); Interest: ($300); Silver Watch: ($10); Plate and Jewerly: ($6); Pleasure Vehicles: ($50).

WARD, JAMES
    Land: 200a. ($800); Slaves: 1 ($400).

WHITE, AUGUSTUS   voter
    Land: 170a. ($340).

WHITE, DAVID, JR.   voter
    Land: 122a. ($444); Interest: ($200).

(White's)

WHITE, DAVID or ESTATE

WHITE, FRANCIS
    Land: 122a. ($144); Slaves: 1 ($450).

WHITE, HENRY, SNR.
    Land: 425a. ($850); Slaves: 6 ($1500).

WHITE, JOSEPH W.   voter
    Land: 157a. ($367).

WHITE, VANN BUREN   voter
    Land: 121a. ($275).

WHITE, WILLIAM
    Land: 210a. ($525); Interest: ($267).

WIGGINS, JAMES (in the army)
    Land: 32a. ($80).

WILLIAM, HENRY H.   voter
    Land: 148a. ($400)

WILLIAM, JAMES L. (in the amry).

WILLIAM, JOSEPH T. (in the amry).

(White's)

Total Taxable Property:

Land: 25,943a. - $96,697

Slaves: 354 - $109,216

Interest received or due: $16,844

Silver Watches: $116

Gold Watches: $180

Piano: 2

Plate and Jewelry: $31

Pleasure Vehicles: $1,325

Household Furniture: $957

Total Value: $225,366

Total number of white voters: 52

Total people listed: 152

State of North Carolina
" Bertie County Court February 1862 ordered that Isaac Piland be appointed to take the tax list in the White District for the year 1862 and that he return the same on or before the second day of May 1862."

                                        Wm P. Gurley
                                        Clerk